PRAISE FOR THIS BOOK

This book comprehensively covers the analytical models and techniques for rating scale analysis. The author uses plain and clear language to explain all the models, equations, and illustrations of rating scale analysis in the book. I appreciate that the author makes the data and all software scripts available.
—Yi-Hsin Chen, *University of South Florida*

This book makes a valuable contribution to the field of rating scale analysis, and one that methodologists in the field of psychometrics should strongly consider.
—Mark Ellickson, *Missouri State University*

Wind takes the complex topic of evaluating rating scales and explains the core issues researchers must address throughout the process.
—Charles P. Kost II, *Colorado Technical University*

This book includes much good content that will help students and researchers in their survey research, along with some great examples.
—Jingshun Zhang, *Florida Gulf Coast University*

QUANTITATIVE APPLICATIONS IN THE SOCIAL SCIENCES

(1) Analysis of Variance, 2nd Edition *Iversen/ Norpoth*
(2) Operations Research Methods *Nagel/Neef*
(3) Causal Modeling, 2nd Edition *Asher*
(4) Tests of Significance *Henkel*
(5) Cohort Analysis, 2nd Edition *Glenn*
(6) Canonical Analysis and Factor Comparison *Levine*
(7) Analysis of Nominal Data, 2nd Edition *Reynolds*
(8) Analysis of Ordinal Data *Hildebrand/Laing/ Rosenthal*
(9) Time Series Analysis, 2nd Edition *Ostrom*
(10) Ecological Inference *Langbein/Lichtman*
(11) Multidimensional Scaling *Kruskal/Wish*
(12) Analysis of Covariance *Wildt/Ahtola*
(13) Introduction to Factor Analysis *Kim/Mueller*
(14) Factor Analysis *Kim/Mueller*
(15) Multiple Indicators *Sullivan/Feldman*
(16) Exploratory Data Analysis *Hartwig/Dearing*
(17) Reliability and Validity Assessment *Carmines/ Zeller*
(18) Analyzing Panel Data *Markus*
(19) Discriminant Analysis *Klecka*
(20) Log-Linear Models *Knoke/Burke*
(21) Interrupted Time Series Analysis *McDowall/ McCleary/Meidinger/Hay*
(22) Applied Regression, 2nd Edition *Lewis-Beck/ Lewis-Beck*
(23) Research Designs *Spector*
(24) Unidimensional Scaling *McIver/Carmines*
(25) Magnitude Scaling *Lodge*
(26) Multiattribute Evaluation *Edwards/Newman*
(27) Dynamic Modeling *Huckfeldt/Kohfeld/Likens*
(28) Network Analysis *Knoke/Kuklinski*
(29) Interpreting and Using Regression *Achen*
(30) Test Item Bias *Osterlind*
(31) Mobility Tables *Hout*
(32) Measures of Association *Liebetrau*
(33) Confirmatory Factor Analysis *Long*
(34) Covariance Structure Models *Long*
(35) Introduction to Survey Sampling, 2nd Edition *Kalton*
(36) Achievement Testing *Bejar*
(37) Nonrecursive Causal Models *Berry*
(38) Matrix Algebra *Namboodiri*
(39) Introduction to Applied Demography *Rives/ Serow*
(40) Microcomputer Methods for Social Scientists, 2nd Edition *Schrodt*
(41) Game Theory *Zagare*
(42) Using Published Data *Jacob*

(43) Bayesian Statistical Inference *Iversen*
(44) Cluster Analysis *Aldenderfer/Blashfield*
(45) Linear Probability, Logit, and Probit Models *Aldrich/Nelson*
(46) Event History and Survival Analysis, 2nd Edition *Allison*
(47) Canonical Correlation Analysis *Thompson*
(48) Models for Innovation Diffusion *Mahajan/ Peterson*
(49) Basic Content Analysis, 2nd Edition *Weber*
(50) Multiple Regression in Practice *Berry/Feldman*
(51) Stochastic Parameter Regression Models *Newbold/Bos*
(52) Using Microcomputers in Research *Madron/ Tate/Brookshire*
(53) Secondary Analysis of Survey Data *Kiecolt/ Nathan*
(54) Multivariate Analysis of Variance *Bray/Maxwell*
(55) The Logic of Causal Order *Davis*
(56) Introduction to Linear Goal Programming *Ignizio*
(57) Understanding Regression Analysis, 2nd Edition *Schroeder/Sjoquist/Stephan*
(58) Randomized Response and Related Methods, 2nd Edition *Fox/Tracy*
(59) Meta-Analysis *Wolf*
(60) Linear Programming *Feiring*
(61) Multiple Comparisons *Klockars/Sax*
(62) Information Theory *Krippendorff*
(63) Survey Questions *Converse/Presser*
(64) Latent Class Analysis *McCutcheon*
(65) Three-Way Scaling and Clustering *Arabie/ Carroll/DeSarbo*
(66) Q Methodology, 2nd Edition *McKeown/Thomas*
(67) Analyzing Decision Making *Louviere*
(68) Rasch Models for Measurement *Andrich*
(69) Principal Components Analysis *Dunteman*
(70) Pooled Time Series Analysis *Sayrs*
(71) Analyzing Complex Survey Data, 2nd Edition *Lee/Forthofer*
(72) Interaction Effects in Multiple Regression, 2nd Edition *Jaccard/Turrisi*
(73) Understanding Significance Testing *Mohr*
(74) Experimental Design and Analysis *Brown/ Melamed*
(75) Metric Scaling *Weller/Romney*
(76) Longitudinal Research, 2nd Edition *Menard*
(77) Expert Systems *Benfer/Brent/Furbee*
(78) Data Theory and Dimensional Analysis *Jacoby*
(79) Regression Diagnostics, 2nd Edition *Fox*
(80) Computer-Assisted Interviewing *Saris*

(81) Contextual Analysis *Iversen*
(82) Summated Rating Scale Construction *Spector*
(83) Central Tendency and Variability *Weisberg*
(84) ANOVA: Repeated Measures *Girden*
(85) Processing Data *Bourque/Clark*
(86) Logit Modeling *DeMaris*
(87) Analytic Mapping and Geographic Databases *Garson/Biggs*
(88) Working With Archival Data *Elder/Pavalko/Clipp*
(89) Multiple Comparison Procedures *Toothaker*
(90) Nonparametric Statistics *Gibbons*
(91) Nonparametric Measures of Association *Gibbons*
(92) Understanding Regression Assumptions *Berry*
(93) Regression With Dummy Variables *Hardy*
(94) Loglinear Models With Latent Variables *Hagenaars*
(95) Bootstrapping *Mooney/Duval*
(96) Maximum Likelihood Estimation *Eliason*
(97) Ordinal Log-Linear Models *Ishii-Kuntz*
(98) Random Factors in ANOVA *Jackson/Brashers*
(99) Univariate Tests for Time Series Models *Cromwell/Labys/Terraza*
(100) Multivariate Tests for Time Series Models *Cromwell/Hannan/Labys/Terraza*
(101) Interpreting Probability Models: Logit, Probit, and Other Generalized Linear Models *Liao*
(102) Typologies and Taxonomies *Bailey*
(103) Data Analysis: An Introduction *Lewis-Beck*
(104) Multiple Attribute Decision Making *Yoon/Hwang*
(105) Causal Analysis With Panel Data *Finkel*
(106) Applied Logistic Regression Analysis, 2nd Edition *Menard*
(107) Chaos and Catastrophe Theories *Brown*
(108) Basic Math for Social Scientists: Concepts *Hagle*
(109) Basic Math for Social Scientists: Problems and Solutions *Hagle*
(110) Calculus *Iversen*
(111) Regression Models: Censored, Sample Selected, or Truncated Data *Breen*
(112) Tree Models of Similarity and Association *Corter*
(113) Computational Modeling *Taber/Timpone*
(114) LISREL Approaches to Interaction Effects in Multiple Regression *Jaccard/Wan*
(115) Analyzing Repeated Surveys *Firebaugh*
(116) Monte Carlo Simulation *Mooney*
(117) Statistical Graphics for Univariate and Bivariate Data *Jacoby*
(118) Interaction Effects in Factorial Analysis of Variance *Jaccard*
(119) Odds Ratios in the Analysis of Contingency Tables *Rudas*

(120) Statistical Graphics for Visualizing Multivariate Data *Jacoby*
(121) Applied Correspondence Analysis *Clausen*
(122) Game Theory Topics *Fink/Gates/Humes*
(123) Social Choice: Theory and Research *Johnson*
(124) Neural Networks *Abdi/Valentin/Edelman*
(125) Relating Statistics and Experimental Design: An Introduction *Levin*
(126) Latent Class Scaling Analysis *Dayton*
(127) Sorting Data: Collection and Analysis *Coxon*
(128) Analyzing Documentary Accounts *Hodson*
(129) Effect Size for ANOVA Designs *Cortina/Nouri*
(130) Nonparametric Simple Regression: Smoothing Scatterplots *Fox*
(131) Multiple and Generalized Nonparametric Regression *Fox*
(132) Logistic Regression: A Primer, 2nd Edition *Pampel*
(133) Translating Questionnaires and Other Research Instruments: Problems and Solutions *Behling/Law*
(134) Generalized Linear Models: A Unified Approach, 2nd Edition *Gill/Torres*
(135) Interaction Effects in Logistic Regression *Jaccard*
(136) Missing Data *Allison*
(137) Spline Regression Models *Marsh/Cormier*
(138) Logit and Probit: Ordered and Multinomial Models *Borooah*
(139) Correlation: Parametric and Nonparametric Measures *Chen/Popovich*
(140) Confidence Intervals *Smithson*
(141) Internet Data Collection *Best/Krueger*
(142) Probability Theory *Rudas*
(143) Multilevel Modeling, 2nd Edition *Luke*
(144) Polytomous Item Response Theory Models *Ostini/Nering*
(145) An Introduction to Generalized Linear Models *Dunteman/Ho*
(146) Logistic Regression Models for Ordinal Response Variables *O'Connell*
(147) Fuzzy Set Theory: Applications in the Social Sciences *Smithson/Verkuilen*
(148) Multiple Time Series Models *Brandt/Williams*
(149) Quantile Regression *Hao/Naiman*
(150) Differential Equations: A Modeling Approach *Brown*
(151) Graph Algebra: Mathematical Modeling With a Systems Approach *Brown*
(152) Modern Methods for Robust Regression *Andersen*
(153) Agent-Based Models, 2nd Edition *Gilbert*
(154) Social Network Analysis, 3rd Edition *Knoke/Yang*
(155) Spatial Regression Models, 2nd Edition *Ward/Gleditsch*

(156) Mediation Analysis *Iacobucci*
(157) Latent Growth Curve Modeling *Preacher/Wichman/MacCallum/Briggs*
(158) Introduction to the Comparative Method With Boolean Algebra *Caramani*
(159) A Mathematical Primer for Social Statistics, 2nd Edition *Fox*
(160) Fixed Effects Regression Models *Allison*
(161) Differential Item Functioning, 2nd Edition *Osterlind/Everson*
(162) Quantitative Narrative Analysis *Franzosi*
(163) Multiple Correspondence Analysis *LeRoux/Rouanet*
(164) Association Models *Wong*
(165) Fractal Analysis *Brown/Liebovitch*
(166) Assessing Inequality *Hao/Naiman*
(167) Graphical Models and the Multigraph Representation for Categorical Data *Khamis*
(168) Nonrecursive Models *Paxton/Hipp/Marquart-Pyatt*
(169) Ordinal Item Response Theory *Van Schuur*
(170) Multivariate General Linear Models *Haase*
(171) Methods of Randomization in Experimental Design *Alferes*
(172) Heteroskedasticity in Regression *Kaufman*
(173) An Introduction to Exponential Random Graph Modeling *Harris*
(174) Introduction to Time Series Analysis *Pickup*
(175) Factorial Survey Experiments *Auspurg/Hinz*

(176) Introduction to Power Analysis: Two-Group Studies *Hedberg*
(177) Linear Regression: A Mathematical Introduction *Gujarati*
(178) Propensity Score Methods and Applications *Bai/Clark*
(179) Multilevel Structural Equation Modeling *Silva/Bosancianu/Littvay*
(180) Gathering Social Network Data *Adams*
(181) Generalized Linear Models for Bounded and Limited Quantitative Variables *Smithson/Shou*
(182) Exploratory Factor Analysis *Finch*
(183) Multidimensional Item Response Theory *Bonifay*
(184) Argument-Based Validation in Testing and Assessment *Chapelle*
(185) Using Time Series to Analyze Long Range Fractal Patterns *Koopmans*
(186) Understanding Correlation Matrices *Hadd/Rodgers*
(187) Rasch Models for Solving Measurement Problems *Engelhard/Wang*
(188) Analyzing Textual Information *Ledolter/VanderVelde*
(189) Confirmatory Factor Analysis *Roos/Bauldry*
(190) Sequence Analysis *Raab/Struffolino*
(191) Applied Bayesian Statistics *Lynch*
(192) Longitudinal Network Models *Duxbury*

SERIES: QUANTITATIVE APPLICATIONS IN THE SOCIAL SCIENCES

Series Editor: Barbara Entwisle, Sociology, *The University of North Carolina at Chapel Hill*

Editorial Board

Richard A. Berk, *Sociology, University of California, Los Angeles*
William D. Berry, *Political Science, Florida State University*
Kenneth A. Bollen, *Sociology, The University of North Carolina at Chapel Hill*
John Fox, Sociology, *McMaster University*
Michael Friendly, *Psychology, York University*
Jacques A. Hagenaars, *Social Sciences, Tilburg University*
Ben B. Hansen, *Statistics, University of Michigan*
Sally Jackson, *Communication, University of Illinois at Urbana-Champaign*
William G. Jacoby, *Political Science, Michigan State University*
Gary King, *Government, Harvard University*
Roger E. Kirk, *Psychology, Baylor University*
Erin Leahey, *Sociology, The University of Arizona*
Michael Lewis-Beck, *Political Science, The University of Iowa*
Tim Liao, Sociology, *University of Illinois at Urbana-Champaign*
Scott Long, *Sociology and Statistics, Indiana University*
Peter Marsden, *Sociology, Harvard University*
Helmut Norpoth, *Political Science, SUNY Stony Brook*
Michael D. Ornstein, *Sociology, York University*
Robert A. Stine, *Statistics, University of Pennsylvania*
Yu Xie, Sociology, *Princeton University*

Exploring Rating Scale Functioning for Survey Research

Exploring Rating Scale Functioning for Survey Research

Stefanie A. Wind
The University of Alabama

Los Angeles | London | New Delhi
Singapore | Washington DC | Melbourne

FOR INFORMATION:

SAGE Publications, Inc.

2455 Teller Road

Thousand Oaks, California 91320

E-mail: order@sagepub.com

SAGE Publications Ltd.

1 Oliver's Yard

55 City Road

London, EC1Y 1SP

United Kingdom

SAGE Publications India Pvt. Ltd.

B 1/I 1 Mohan Cooperative Industrial Area

Mathura Road, New Delhi 110 044

India

SAGE Publications Asia-Pacific Pte. Ltd.

18 Cross Street #10-10/11/12

China Square Central

Singapore 048423

Acquisitions Editor: Helen Salmon
Product Associate: Yumna Samnie
Production Editor: Vijayakumar
Copy Editor: Christobel Colleen Hopman
Typesetter: TNQ Technologies
Proofreader: Benny Willy Stephen
Indexer: TNQ Technologies
Cover Designer: Candice Harman
Marketing Manager: Victoria Velasquez

Copyright © 2023 by SAGE Publications, Inc.

All rights reserved. Except as permitted by US copyright law, no part of this work may be reproduced or distributed in any form or by any means, or stored in a database or retrieval system, without permission in writing from the publisher.

All third-party trademarks referenced or depicted herein are included solely for the purpose of illustration and are the property of their respective owners. Reference to these trademarks in no way indicates any relationship with, or endorsement by, the trademark owner.

Printed in the United States of America

Library of Congress Cataloging-in-Publication Data

Names: Wind, Stefanie A. (Anne), author.

Title: Exploring rating scale functioning for survey research / Stefanie A. Wind, The University of Alabama.

Identifiers: LCCN 2022047111 | ISBN 9781071855379 (paperback) | ISBN 9781071855409 (adobe pdf) | ISBN 9781071855386 (epub) | ISBN 9781071855393 (epub)

Subjects: LCSH: Psychometrics. | Invariant measures. | Rasch models. | Psychology–Statistical methods. | Social sciences–Statistical methods. | Social surveys.

Classification: LCC BF39 .W563 2023 | DDC 150.28/7–dc23/eng/20221020

LC record available at https://lccn.loc.gov/2022047111

This book is printed on acid-free paper.

22 23 24 25 26 10 9 8 7 6 5 4 3 2 1

BRIEF CONTENTS

Series Editor Introduction		xiv
Acknowledgments		xvi
About the Author		xvii
List of Acronyms		xviii
Accompanying Website		xix
1	What Is Rating Scale Analysis?	1
2	Rasch Models for Rating Scale Analysis	19
3	Illustration of Rating Scale Analysis With Polytomous Rasch Models	48
4	Non-Rasch IRT Models for Rating Scale Analysis	87
5	Nonparametric Measurement Models for Rating Scale Analysis	125
6	Summary and Resources for Further Study	150
Tables		171
Glossary		181
References		185
Index		193

DETAILED CONTENTS

Series Editor Introduction	xiv
Acknowledgments	xvi
About the Author	xvii
List of Acronyms	xviii
Accompanying Website	xix

1 What Is Rating Scale Analysis? — **1**

What Is Item Response Theory? — 2

IRT for Rating Scale Data — *4*

What Is Rating Scale Analysis? — 5

How Is Rating Scale Analysis Different From Other Survey Analyses? — *5*

What Are the Requirements for Rating Scale Analysis? — *8*

How Should Researchers Select a Model for Rating Scale Analysis? — 11

What Can Be Learned From Rating Scale Analysis? — *15*

What Will This Book Help Researchers Do With Their Data? — 15

Introduction to Example Data — 17

Resources for Further Study — 18

2 Rasch Models for Rating Scale Analysis — **19**

What Is Rasch Measurement Theory? — 19

What Are Rasch Models? — *20*

Polytomous Rasch Models for Rating Scale Analysis — *23*

Why Are Polytomous Rasch Models Useful for Rating Scale Analysis? — *25*

Rasch Models for Rating Scale Analysis — 27

Rating Scale Model (RSM) — *27*

Application of the RSM to the CES-D Scale Data — *28*

Preliminary Analysis: Model-Data Fit — *29*

Overall RSM Results — *34*

Partial Credit Model (PCM)	38
Application of the PCM to the CES-D Data	*40*
Extending the Rating Scale and Partial Credit Models: The Many-Facet Rasch Model (MFRM)	41
Application of the PC-MFRM to the CES-D Data	*44*
Chapter Summary	45

3 Illustration of Rating Scale Analysis With Polytomous Rasch Models **48**

Rating Scale Analysis With the Rating Scale Model	48
Rating Scale Category Ordering	*50*
Rating Scale Category Precision	*54*
Rating Scale Category Comparability	*60*
Rating Scale Analysis With the Partial Credit Model	61
Category Ordering Indices	*61*
Rating Scale Category Precision	*66*
Rating Scale Category Comparability	*70*
Rating Scale Analyses With the Partial Credit Many-Facet Rasch Model	71
Category Ordering Indices	*72*
Rating Scale Category Precision	*74*
Chapter Summary	82
Appendix	84

4 Non-Rasch IRT Models for Rating Scale Analysis **87**

Rating Scale Analysis Using Polytomous IRT Models With Slope Parameters	88
Generalized Partial Credit Model	*90*
Overall Model Results	93
Rating Scale Category Ordering	96
Average Participant Locations Within Rating Scale Categories	*96*
Logit-Scale Location Estimates of Item-Specific Rating Scale Category Thresholds	*97*
Ordering of Item-Specific Category Probability Curves	*98*
Rating Scale Category Precision	99
Distance Between Item-Specific Threshold Location Estimates on the Logit Scale	*99*
Distinct Item-Specific Category Probability Curves	*100*
Graded Response Model	104
Illustration of Rating Scale Analysis With the Graded Response Model	*107*

Overall Model Results	109
Rating Scale Category Ordering	110
Average Participant Locations Within Item-Specific Rating Scale Categories for Individual Items	*111*
Rating Scale Category Precision	111
Distance Between Rating Scale Category Threshold Estimates on the Logit Scale for Individual Items	*111*
Plots of Cumulative Category Probabilities for Individual Items	*112*
Plots of Individual Category Probabilities for Individual Items	*117*
Chapter Summary	117
Appendix	119

5 Nonparametric Measurement Models for Rating Scale Analysis **125**

Mokken Scale Analysis	126
Overview of Mokken Models for Rating Scale Data	127
Polytomous Monotone Homogeneity Model	*127*
Polytomous Double Monotonicity Model	*134*
Rating Scale Category Ordering	138
Average Participant Restscores Within Rating Scale Categories for Individual Items	*138*
Counts of Item-Specific Violations of Category Monotonicity	*139*
Graphical Displays of Cumulative Category Monotonicity for Individual Items	*139*
Rating Scale Category Precision	140
Distinct Cumulative Category Probabilities for Individual Items	*140*
Discriminating Item-Specific Cumulative Category Probabilities	*144*
Chapter Summary	145
Appendix	147

6 Summary and Resources for Further Study **150**

What Is Rating Scale Analysis?	150
Summary of Previous Chapters	151
How Should a Researcher Select a Model for Rating Scale Analysis?	153
Overall Modeling Goals	*153*
Practical Goals for Rating Scale Analysis	*154*
Considerations Related to Audience	*156*

Practical Takeaways: How Can a Researcher Use
Results From Rating Scale Analysis? 156
What Should I Do If My Scale Categories
Are Disordered? *156*
What Should I Do If My Scale Categories
Are Imprecise? *158*
How Do I Know If My Neutral Category
Is Meaningful? *159*
Resources for Further Study 160
Methodological Research on Rating Scale Analysis *160*
Examples of Applications of Rating Scale Analysis
to Real Survey Data *160*
Appendix 163

Tables **171**

Glossary **181**

References **185**

Index **193**

SERIES EDITOR INTRODUCTION

Many are concerned with reliability, validity, and fairness of measures collected in survey research. In **Evaluating Rating Scale Functioning for Survey Research**, Stefanie A. Wind addresses a related issue: the performance of rating scales. This includes ordering of response categories, precision in distinguishing respondents with respect to the construct of interest, and comparability across components of the overall measure or across subgroups of respondents. A contributor to the methodology of rating scale analysis herself, Professor Wind is ideally placed to bring these methods to a larger audience.

Surveys serve as a workhorse of data collection in the social and behavioral sciences. Items with ordered response categories are common in survey research. For example, respondents might be asked how much they agree with certain statements (1 = strongly agree to 5 = strongly disagree), how much trust they have in certain institutions (1 = very much to 4 = not at all), or their willingness to intervene in certain situations (1 = very likely to 5 = very unlikely). Do responses of "neither agree nor disagree" truly fall in between "agree" and "disagree"? How large are the differences between categories of response? How well do they distinguish between respondents? This volume is the first to introduce the evaluation of rating scales to an audience of survey researchers.

The methods introduced in **Evaluating Rating Scale Functioning for Survey Research** have some requirements that focus its use. First, there need to be sufficient items to measure a unidimensional construct reliably, preferably five items, even better to have ten. Second, items must have at least three or more ordered response categories. Third, sample size should be at least 100. The second and third requirements are easily met in survey research. The first is more challenging, but there are many scales that meet it, such as, the Center for Epidemiological Studies Depression (CES-D) Scale, Everett's Social and Economic Conservatism Scale, Sampson's Collective Efficacy Scale, and various measures of trust in institutions.

xiv

Evaluating Rating Scale Functioning for Survey Research presents three categories of methods: Rasch models; non-Rasch Item Response Theory (IRT) models; and nonparametric models. Rasch models are used to evaluate characteristics of the data with respect to a theory of measurement, which assumes invariant measurement, local independence, and unidimensionality. Professor Wind grounds readers with a full discussion of the Rasch approach and illustrates with applications of the Rating Scale Model, Partial Credit Model and the Partial Credit Many-Facet Rasch Model. Non-Rasch models are used to describe characteristics of the data when, for whatever reason, researchers do not need or wish to establish a single item and person hierarchy to represent a construct. Professor Wind presents and illustrates two non-Rasch IRT models (the Generalized Partial Credit Model and the Graded Response Model) and two nonparametric models from Mokken Scale Analysis (the Polytomous Monotone Homogeneity Model and the Double Monotonicity Model). She uses the CES-D to demonstrate the application of all of these models and the interpretation of tabular results as well as graphical displays.

Although readers already familiar with Rasch models will gain the most from **Evaluating Rating Scale Functioning in Survey Research**, Professor Wind provides much of the needed scaffolding for those without this background. In Chapter 2, she introduces the Rasch model and a fully worked-out application using the Rating Scale Model. Subsequent chapters build on this foundational material, each one addressing the benefits offered by a particular method in relation to the others that preceded it. The concluding chapter summarizes this helpful guidance. With this volume in hand, even those relatively new to psychological measurement theory will be able to conduct and interpret the results of rating scale analysis. The benefits will accrue to all interested in survey measurement.

Tutorials, datasets, and software code (R and Facets) to accompany the book are available on the book's website at **https://study.sagepub. com/researchmethods/qass/wind-exploring-rating-scale-functio**ning.

Barbara Entwisle
Series Editor

ACKNOWLEDGMENTS

I would like to thank Barbara Entwisle, the Series Editor, for her constant support, encouragement, and constructive comments as I prepared this book. This manuscript has been much improved by Barbara's input, and I am grateful to have had the chance to work with her on this project. I would also like to thank the reviewers whose comments and suggestions helped to improve it. I would also like to acknowledge my colleagues and students who provided feedback on early versions of the book proposal and chapters, including Dr. Wenjing Guo and Dr. Ryan Cook at the University of Alabama.

SAGE and the author are grateful for feedback from the following reviewers in the development of this text:

- Kelly D. Bradley, *University of Kentucky*
- Yi-Hsin Chen, *University of South Florida*
- Mark Ellickson, *Missouri State University*
- John Fox, *McMaster University*
- A. Corinne Huggins-Manley, *University of Florida*
- Charles P. Kost II, *Colorado Technical University*
- Vanessa L. Malcarne, *San Diego State University*
- Anne Traynor, *Purdue University*
- Dana Linnell Wanzer, *University of Wisconsin-Stout*
- Jingshun Zhang, *Florida Gulf Coast University*

ABOUT THE AUTHOR

Stefanie A. Wind is an Associate Professor of Educational Measurement at the University of Alabama. Her primary research interests include the exploration of methodological issues in the field of educational measurement, with emphases on methods related to rater-mediated assessments, rating scales, Rasch models, item response theory models, and nonparametric item response theory, as well as applications of these methods to substantive areas related to education.

LIST OF ACRONYMS

CES-D scale	Center for Epidemiological Studies Depression scale
DMM	Double Monotonicity Model
GPCM	Generalized Partial Credit Model
GRM	Graded Response Model
IIO	Invariant Item Ordering
IRF	Item Response Function
IRT	Item Response Theory
ISRF	Item Step Response Function
MFRM	Many-Facet Rasch Model
MHM	Monotone Homogeneity Model
PC-MFRM	Partial Credit Many-Facet Rasch Model
PCM	Partial Credit Model
RSM	Rating Scale Model
SD	Standard Deviation
SE	Standard Error

ACCOMPANYING WEBSITE

Tutorials, datasets, and software code (R and Facets) to accompany the book are available on the book's website at **https://study.sagepub.com/ researchmethods/qass/wind-exploring-rating-scale-functioning**.

1 WHAT IS RATING SCALE ANALYSIS?

The central topic of this volume is *rating scale functioning*. Rating scale functioning refers to the degree to which ordinal rating scales with three or more categories, such as Likert-type rating scales used in attitude surveys, can be interpreted and used in a psychometrically sound way. Researchers who are concerned with rating scale functioning evaluate their rating scale data for properties such as those listed in Table 1.1.

First, rating scale functioning is concerned with *rating scale category ordering*. When rating scale categories are functioning well, higher categories in a rating scale should reflect higher levels of the construct being measured. For example, in a scale designed to measure empathy, participants who *Strongly Agree* with statements asking whether they exhibit empathetic behaviors should have higher levels of empathy than participants who *Agree* with those statements. Next, *rating scale category precision* refers to the degree to which individual rating scale categories make meaningful distinctions between participants with respect to the construct. When rating scales function well, each category reflects a unique level of the construct. For example, there should be a meaningful difference in the level of empathy between participants who *Strongly Agree* and those who *Agree* with survey items. Finally, *rating scale category comparability* analyses help researchers investigate whether rating scale categories have a similar interpretation across assessment components or subgroups of participants. For example, the

Table 1.1   Indices Used in Rating Scale Analysis

Rating Scale Properties	*Guiding Question for Rating Scale Analysis*
Rating scale category ordering	To what extent do higher rating scale categories indicate higher locations on the construct?
Rating scale category precision	To what extent do individual rating scale categories reflect distinct ranges on the construct?
Rating scale category comparability	To what extent do rating scale categories have a similar interpretation and use across assessment components or subgroups of participants?

2

difference in the level of the empathy required to *Strongly Agree* and *Agree* should be similar across participants with different levels of education. There are many analytic techniques through which researchers can explore rating scale functioning. However, methods based on Rasch models and item response theory (IRT) models are particularly suited to this approach. In this book, we explore methods for examining rating scale functioning using these methods.

The purpose of this book is to provide readers with an overview of rating scale analysis, choices involved in rating scale analysis, and practical guidance on how to conduct such analyses with their own survey data. The analyses are based on Rasch models and IRT models, with some references to classical test theory to highlight the advantages of the Rasch and IRT approaches.

The organizing principle for this book is that rating scale functioning must be examined each time a survey is administered before inferences can be made from participant responses. Currently, most of the information about rating scale analysis is contained in a substantially longer and technically sophisticated book (Wright & Masters, 1982) or in a few select chapters in longer books (e.g., Engelhard & Wind, 2018) and articles (Linacre, 2002; Wind, 2014) whose target audience is methodologists in the area of psychometrics. The current volume is targeted to a wider audience, and readers need only basic training in psychometrics and familiarity with Rasch and IRT approaches in order to understand and apply all of the concepts. Readers who are beginners in psychometrics can focus on the interpretation and practical use of rating scale analysis methods.

What Is Item Response Theory?

IRT is a paradigm for the development, analysis, and evaluation of measurement instruments (e.g., surveys or tests) for latent variables (i.e., constructs), such as attitudes, abilities, or achievement levels in the social sciences. IRT is sometimes referred to as latent trait theory, strong true score theory, or modern measurement theory, among other names (Embretson & Reise, 2000). IRT is a broad framework in which numerous models are available for different kinds of measurement tools and assessment contexts. Each model is characterized by assumptions that are reflected in model parameters and formulations. These differences have implications for the information that each model provides about participants, items, and latent variables. For example, many IRT models assume or require approximate *unidimensionality*. In the context of IRT, unidimensionality means that a single latent variable can be used to explain most of the variation in the item responses of interest.

The basic idea underlying unidimensional IRT models is that latent variables can be expressed using a single linear continuum on which participants and items have unique locations.

For example, in an educational assessment designed to measure student achievement in physical science, students whose understanding of physical science concepts are relatively advanced would have higher locations on the construct compared to students whose understanding of physical science concepts are less advanced. Likewise, items that require more proficiency in physical science to produce a correct response (i.e., difficult items) would have higher locations on the construct compared to items that require less proficiency in physical science to produce a correct response (i.e., easy items). As another example, in a measure of depression, participants with more severe depressive symptoms would have higher locations on the construct compared to participants with less severe depressive symptoms. Items that reflect more frequent or severe depressive symptoms would have higher locations compared to items that reflect less severe symptoms.

Figure 1.1 illustrates the concept of a latent variable expressed as a linear continuum. The horizontal double-ended arrow represents the latent variable (e.g., depression) as a unidimensional continuum ranging from low (e.g., low levels of depression) to high (e.g., high levels of depression). Three participants are shown above the continuum and three items are shown below the continuum, with locations indicated using vertical lines. Participant A has the lowest location (e.g., lowest level of depression), followed by Participant B, followed by Participant C, who has the highest location (e.g., highest level of depression). Likewise, Item 1 has the lowest location (this item requires minimal

Figure 1.1 Illustration of Participant and Item Locations on a Latent Variable

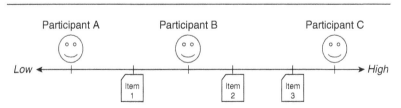

depression for positive responses), followed by Item 2, followed by Item 3, which has the highest location (this item requires severe depression for positive responses).

IRT models describe the probability for a certain type of response (e.g., an accurate response to a multiple-choice item in an educational assessment or a rating of "*Strongly Agree*" to an item in an attitude survey) as a function of the difference between participant locations and item locations on this linear continuum. For example, in Figure 1.1, Participant C would be expected to respond positively to all three items because Participant C's location exceeds those of the items. In contrast, Participant B would be expected to respond positively to Item 1, but not Item 2 or Item 3, whose locations exceed that of Participant B. Participant A would not be expected to respond positively to any of the items.

When there is evidence of acceptable fit between the responses and the model assumptions or requirements (i.e., good model-data fit), the participant and item location estimates can be interpreted as location estimates on a common linear scale that represents the latent variable. This common metric for participants and items is a major advantage of IRT beyond scaling techniques that focus on the decomposition of variance in number-correct or average scores, such as classical test theory (CTT; Crocker & Algina, 1986; Gulliksen, 1950).

IRT for Rating Scale Data

A popular use of IRT is to analyze data from measurement instruments that include rating scales, such as attitude surveys with Likert-type response scales (Likert, 1932). There are a number of IRT models that can be usefully applied to multicategory (i.e., polytomous) data, including the Rating Scale Model (Andrich, 1978), the Partial Credit Model (Masters, 1982), the Generalized Partial Credit Model (Muraki, 1997), the Graded Response Model (Samejima, 1969, 1997), and models from Mokken Scale Analysis (Mokken, 1971); each of these models will be discussed in turn later in this volume. When they are applied to rating scale data, these models provide information with which researchers can evaluate psychometric properties, compare participant and item locations on the construct, and use the results to inform the revision, interpretation, and use of measurement instruments for research and practice. Importantly, IRT models also provide a variety of tools that can be used to conduct rating scale analysis.

What Is Rating Scale Analysis?

Rating scale analysis is a procedure for evaluating rating scale functioning in item response data that includes participant responses in three or more ordered categories (e.g., Likert-type responses) for evidence of useful psychometric properties at the level of individual rating scale categories. To illustrate the concept of rating scale functioning, Figure 1.2 illustrates a typical Likert-type rating scale with five ordered categories. This figure has a similar interpretation to Figure 1.1, but it illustrates the locations of *rating scale categories* on a latent variable. The horizontal double-ended arrow represents a latent variable (e.g., empathy) as a unidimensional continuum ranging from low (e.g., low levels of empathy) to high (e.g., high levels of empathy). Below the arrow, five ordered rating scale categories are shown, ranging from *Strongly Disagree* to *Strongly Agree*. Thick, evenly spaced vertical lines show the four transition points ("thresholds"; τ_k) that correspond to the five adjacent rating scale categories. The location of each threshold on the latent variable is marked with a circle. The thresholds are monotonically nondecreasing as the latent variable progresses from low to high (i.e., $\tau_1 \leq \tau_2 \leq \tau_3 \leq \tau_4$), such that higher levels of the latent variable (e.g., more empathy) would be required to provide a rating in higher categories.

How Is Rating Scale Analysis Different From Other Survey Analyses?

Survey researchers frequently evaluate their data for evidence of validity, reliability, and fairness. These investigations often draw on methods such as factor analysis, internal consistency statistics

Figure 1.2 Illustration of Evenly Spaced, Monotonic, Ordinal Rating Scale Categories

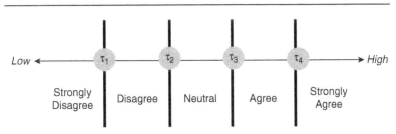

(e.g., alpha), and IRT analyses. Most routine survey analyses focus on *overall item difficulty estimates,* which assume that rating scales can be interpreted as they are illustrated in Figure 1.2. When researchers use these analyses, they assume that the ordinal categories in a rating scale are evenly spaced with respect to the latent variable (e.g., the difference in the level of empathy required to respond in *Strongly Agree* and *Agree* is the same for responses to Item 1 and Item 2) and that increasing categories reflect increasing levels of the latent variable (e.g., responses in the *Neutral* category always reflect higher levels of empathy than responses in the *Disagree* category). If these properties hold, researchers can make meaningful comparisons between participant responses to different items, and across subgroups of participants (e.g., gender subgroups) with regard to the interpretation of the scale categories. Moreover, evidence of acceptable rating scale functioning provides support for interpreting overall item-level analyses and total score analyses related to validity, reliability, and fairness.

Rather than assuming the properties illustrated in Figure 1.2 hold in all situations, rating scale analysis uses indices from IRT models to empirically explore the structure of ordinal rating scales. The purpose of such analyses is to ensure a meaningful interpretation of responses within and across components of a scale and subgroups of participants. For example, rating scale analyses could help researchers identify a scenario such as the one illustrated in Figure 1.3 (discussed next).

Figure 1.3 shows the rating scale structure for three items from a hypothetical survey. For Item 1, rating scale analysis may reveal that the categories are evenly spaced and monotonically nondecreasing as the latent variable progresses from low to high. However, for Item 2, *Strongly Disagree* and *Agree* represent wider ranges of the latent variable compared to *Disagree, Neutral,* and *Strongly Agree.* In addition, the relative distance between category thresholds is not consistent across the scale. For Item 3, the category spacing is different still from that of Item 1 and Item 2. Moreover, the category *ordering* is also different from that of the first two items: For Item 3, responding in the *Disagree* category requires higher levels of the latent variable (e.g., more empathy) than responding in the *Neutral* category, such that $\tau_3 < \tau_2$, whereas the opposite order is true for Item 1 and Item 2. Suffice it to say, it would be difficult to justify interpreting participant responses to Item 3 in the same way as their responses to Item 1 and Item 2.

Rather than focusing on total scores (as in classical test theory) or on overall item difficulty or discrimination parameters (as in many polytomous IRT analyses), rating scale analysis focuses on examining the degree

Figure 1.3 Illustration of Different Rating Scale Structures for Individual Items

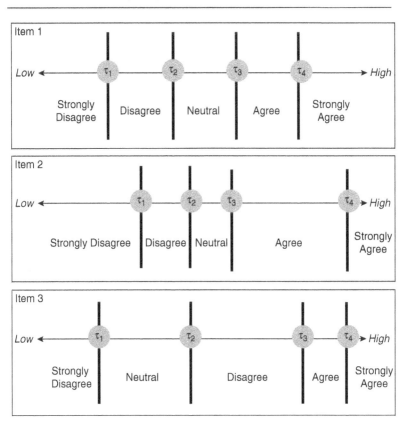

to which the *individual categories* in an ordinal rating scale have a meaningful interpretation that is consistent across elements of the assessment procedure, such as across items, persons, or subgroups of items or persons. This information is important because evidence of acceptable rating scale functioning ensures meaningful interpretation of the directionality of rating scales, informs the interpretation of differences between categories, and ensures a comparable interpretation of categories between items, components of a scale, or subgroups of items or persons. In summary, rating scale analysis supplements routine survey analyses related to validity, reliability, and fairness to help survey researchers ensure that their rating scales have meaningful interpretations.

8

What Are the Requirements for Rating Scale Analysis?

Rating scale analyses can be conducted on item responses across a range of survey research applications designed to measure unidimensional constructs using ordinal rating scales.[1] There are no universal requirements for the maximum number of rating scale categories, minimum sample sizes for persons or items, or the proportion of missing data that always make a dataset eligible for rating scale analysis. However, each of these issues is important and should be considered before conducting rating scale analysis. This section provides guidance on practical considerations related to each of these topics.

Number of Rating Scale Categories

Rating scale analysis can be conducted when rating scales include three or more ordered categories (Wright & Masters, 1982). Examination of survey research literature reveals that researchers tend to disagree about the appropriate maximum length for collecting useful data from survey instruments in general (e.g., Borgers et al., 2004; DeCastellarnau, 2018; Krosnick et al., 2002; Linacre, 2002; Weijters et al., 2010). Similarly, there is no universal maximum value for the number of categories that is appropriate for conducting rating scale analysis. However, there are some general guidelines that researchers can use to determine whether their scale length may be appropriate for rating scale analysis.

Technically, there is no upper limit to the number of scale categories that could be included in rating scale analyses, and researchers could conduct the analyses included in this book on instruments with many rating scale categories, such as Everett's (2013) Social and Economic Conservatism Scale, whose rating scale categories range from 0 to 100. However, there are several practical challenges with long scales. First, if a scale includes many categories, it may be unlikely that there will be enough responses in each category to meaningfully interpret rating scale analysis indicators. This challenge is particularly relevant with small samples, where there may not be sufficient variation within a sample to identify participants at each level of the scale. For example, as will be

---

[1]Rating scale analysis has not yet been considered in the context of multidimensional IRT. However, analysts can apply the techniques illustrated throughout this book to their multidimensional measures by analyzing item responses for each construct separately.

discussed in Chapter 3, one potential cause for disordered categories is a relatively low frequency of observations within a category. In addition, the volume of information that rating scale analysis provides is directly related to the number of categories. Interpreting and using information about rating scale ordering, precision, and comparability for many categories across multiple items may not be practical in all survey research contexts.

The perspective taken in this book is that the number of categories that are suitable for rating scale analysis varies across contexts. Researchers should rely on guidance from the literature, practical experience with their population(s) of interest, and empirical evidence from rating scale analysis methods to determine how many categories are appropriate for their rating scales and subsequent rating scale analyses. The techniques presented in this book provide practical tools with which researchers can empirically evaluate the effectiveness and contribution of each category to a measurement procedure. As we will see throughout the book, rating scale analysis helps researchers use empirical evidence to determine whether more or fewer rating scale categories may be needed in a survey research context and whether this number should be fixed or can vary across items. In addition, rating scale analysis provides empirical evidence to support the use or omission of neutral categories. These issues are considered throughout the volume, and Chapter 6 provides a specific discussion on decisions related to combining or omitting categories based on the results from rating scale analysis.

Participant Sample Size

Sample size requirements for rating scale analysis are directly tied to the modeling choices that researchers make and their plans for statistical tests that they will conduct using scores from the measurement instrument. Among the models considered in this book, those based on nonparametric IRT (see Chapter 5) are the least stringent in sample size requirements (some researchers have reported these analyses with as few as 30 participants), while those based on IRT models with item discrimination parameters, such as the Generalized Partial Credit Model (see Chapter 4), require the largest samples (usually at least 100 or more participants). Methods based on Rasch models (see Chapters 2 and 3) require moderate sample sizes that are generally attainable in most survey research settings (although larger samples are preferred, samples of around 50 participants are sufficient for many purposes, see Linacre, 1994).

10

Item Sample Size

Minimum sample sizes for items in rating scale analysis also reflect item sample size requirements for the models used to conduct those analyses. For Rasch models (see Chapters 2 and 3), item and person sample size requirements are symmetric: The precision of information about people depends on the number of items (and the number of categories), and the precision of information about items depends on the number of people. Because measurement models are not statistical significance tests, it is not possible to conduct a traditional power analysis (Cohen, 1969) to identify an exact minimum sample size for the number of items in an instrument for rating scale analysis. Similar to recommendations for the maximum number of categories in a rating scale, it is not straightforward to provide a critical value or equation with which to identify the minimum number of items. In my experience conducting rating scale analysis on scales in a variety of disciplinary areas, including counseling (Cook et al., 2021), empathy (Wind et al., 2018), language learning (Wind et al., 2019), learning motivation (Wang & Wind, 2020), music performance (Wesolowski et al., 2016), and teacher evaluation (Wind, Tsai, et al., 2018), I have found that scales consisting of around ten or more items tend to exhibit strong overall psychometric properties (e.g., high values of reliability coefficients) while also providing a manageable amount of information about rating scale functioning. Reflecting this experience, the example used in this volume is a version of the Center for Epidemiological Studies Depression (CES-D) scale (discussed later in this chapter) that consists of ten items. I recommend that researchers who have shorter instruments still conduct rating scale analysis; the techniques included in this book will provide useful information about rating scale functioning that can be interpreted in the same way as with longer instruments. However, analysts should keep in mind that few items may negatively impact the overall reliability of the instrument and precision of information that can be gleaned about participants. Likewise, scales with many items can also pose psychometric challenges and impact data quality due to issues such as participant fatigue.

Missing Data

Researchers who conduct surveys often encounter missing data (Bodner, 2006), which occur for various reasons (Little & Rubin, 2002). The choice of model for rating scale analysis determines how missing data can be handled. Among the models included in this book, those based on Rasch measurement theory (see Chapter 2) are particularly amenable to missing data. Specifically, Rasch models can be applied when data are missing as long as there are common observations with which to "link" participants across items and to "link" items across participants (Schumacker, 1999). For example, if participants respond to items in common with other participants, Rasch models can provide location estimates for participants who have not responded to all of the items in the instrument. The same is true for items: Rasch models can provide item location estimates even when some participants have not responded to the item. In contrast, researchers who use non-Rasch IRT models (see Chapter 4) and nonparametric IRT models (see Chapter 5) for rating scale analysis typically impute new values for missing responses before applying the model (Hagedoorn et al., 2018; van der Ark & Sijtsma, 2005).[2]

Relatedly, rating scale analyses should only be conducted on meaningful item responses. For example, some survey instruments allow participants to indicate that an item is not applicable or that they have no opinion about the content in an item. Such response options usually cannot be meaningfully placed within the ordinal rating scale. As a result, they should be treated as missing data and not included in the analysis. Along the same lines, response patterns that reflect careless responding should be handled following best practices in survey research (Arias et al., 2020; Goldammer et al., 2020) and generally should not be included in rating scale analyses.

How Should Researchers Select a Model for Rating Scale Analysis?

This book presents rating scale analysis methods based on several IRT models. Each of the models discussed in this book offers valuable information that can help researchers evaluate their survey instruments from the perspective of rating scale analysis. However, the models have some important differences in the types of data that can be modeled, how they reflect different overall modeling goals, and how they reflect goals specific to rating scale analysis. Table 1.2 provides an overview of these characteristics for the models used in this book. We will refer to

---

[2]There has been some preliminary research on using nonparametric IRT models with missing data that does not require imputation methods (Wind, 2020; Wind & Patil, 2016), but these techniques have not been considered in the context of rating scale analysis.

Table 1.2 Overview of Models for Rating Scale Analysis

| Considerations for Survey Research | | Rasch Models (Chapters 2 and 3) | | | | Parametric Non-Rasch Models (Chapter 4) | | Nonparametric Item Response Models (Chapter 5) |
| | | | | Many-Facet Rasch (MFR) Model | | Generalized | | |
		Rating Scale Model	Partial Credit Model	Rating Scale Many-Facet Rasch Model	Partial Credit Many-Facet Rasch Model	Partial Credit Model	Graded Response Model	Mokken Scale Analysis
Types of Data	Response scale includes three or more ordered categories	X	X	X	X	X	X	X
	Response scale varies across items		X		X	X	X	
Overall Modeling Goals	To evaluate survey data for adherence to fundamental measurement requirements (unidimensionality, local independence, invariance)	X	X	X	X			X

(Continued)

		1	2	3	4	5	6	7
	To obtain linear-scale estimates of item, person, and other facet locations	X	X	X	X	X	X	
	To estimate person and item locations controlling for context-specific explanatory variables			X	X			
	To estimate person and item locations controlling for differences in item slopes					X	X	X
Practical Goals for Rating Scale Analysis	To evaluate rating scale functioning for an entire set of items, without distinguishing between individual items	X		X				
	To evaluate rating scale functioning				X			

(Continued)

Table 1.2 Overview of Models for Rating Scale Analysis *(Continued)*

| | Rasch Models (Chapters 2 and 3) | | | | Parametric Non-Rasch Models (Chapter 4) | | Nonparametric Item Response Models (Chapter 5) |
| | | | Many-Facet Rasch (MFR) Model | | | | |
Considerations for Survey Research	*Rating Scale Model*	*Partial Credit Model*	*Rating Scale Many-Facet Rasch Model*	*Partial Credit Many-Facet Rasch Model*	*Generalized Partial Credit Model*	*Graded Response Model*	*Mokken Scale Analysis*
specific to explanatory variables in an assessment procedure (e.g., person subgroups or item subsets)							
To evaluate rating scale functioning specific to each item		X		X	X	X	X
To evaluate category ordering	X	X	X	X	X		
To evaluate category precision	X	X	X	X	X	X	X

Table 1.2 throughout the book as we consider rating scale analysis techniques based on each model. We revisit the topic of model selection for rating scale analysis in Chapter 6.

What Can Be Learned From Rating Scale Analysis?

Put simply, rating scale analysis helps analysts learn about the quality of their rating scales from a psychometric perspective. Rating scale functioning is an empirical property of item response data that needs to be explored each time a survey is administered. Rather than assuming that rating scale categories are ordered as expected, describe unique ranges of the latent variable, and have comparable interpretations for all items and participants, rating scale analysis helps researchers verify these properties and identify directions for further research or improvement to a measurement instrument. Rating scale analysis supplements other psychometric analyses to help researchers ensure that they can meaningfully interpret the results from participant responses to ordinal rating scales.

What Will This Book Help Researchers Do With Their Data?

This book aims to help researchers identify useful techniques for exploring rating scale functioning in their data and to provide guidance in interpreting the results, along with resources for applying these analyses. Specifically, this book will help researchers use polytomous IRT models to empirically gauge the degree to which participant responses to ordinal rating scales display evidence of psychometrically defensible rating scale functioning. Such information is essential for the meaningful interpretation and use of rating scale data.

Recent developments in statistical software have made rating scale analysis relatively straightforward for analysts who have a basic working knowledge of psychometrics and psychometric software. This book includes online supplemental materials at **https://study.sagepub.com/ researchmethods/qass/wind-exploring-rating-scale-functioning** that demonstrate the application of rating scale analysis techniques using R packages (R Core Team, 2021), Winsteps (Linacre, 2016), and Facets (Linacre, 2020). Readers can adapt the provided code for use with their own data.

The remaining chapters are organized as follows. Chapter 2 introduces polytomous models for exploring rating scale functioning based on Rasch measurement theory (Rasch, 1960); these models have several useful properties that make them particularly well suited to rating scale

16

Table 1.3 CES-D Scale Item Stems

Item Number	Item Stem
1	I was bothered by things that usually don't bother me.
2	I did not feel like eating; my appetite was poor.
3	I felt that I could not shake off the blues even with help from my family or friends.
4[a]	I felt I was just as good as other people.
5	I had trouble keeping my mind on what I was doing.
6	I felt depressed.
7	I felt that everything I did was an effort.
8[a]	I felt hopeful about the future.
9	I thought my life had been a failure.
10	I felt fearful.
11	My sleep was restless.
12[a]	I was happy.
13	I talked less than usual.
14	I felt lonely.
15	People were unfriendly.
16[a]	I enjoyed life.
17	I had crying spells.
18	I felt sad.
19	I felt that people dislike me.
20	I could not get "going."

[a]These items are intended to be reverse-coded prior to analysis.

analysis. Chapter 3 continues the discussion of Rasch models for rating scale analysis by demonstrating the application of these models to explore rating scale functioning, along with the interpretation of the results. Chapter 3 includes step-by-step examples and illustrations of rating scale analysis techniques that are supplemented with online resources for applying the analyses using statistical software. Chapter 4 provides a theoretical overview of several popular non-Rasch IRT models that can be used to explore rating scale functioning. Chapter 5 presents a nonparametric approach to rating scale analysis. In Chapter 6, the book concludes with a summary of the topics covered in previous chapters, a discussion of practical choices and considerations for rating scale analysis, and resources for further study.

Introduction to Example Data

To illustrate the application of the methods discussed in this book, example analyses and results will be provided using analyses of data based on an administration of the CES-D scale (Radloff, 1977) as reported by Donny et al. (2015). The CES-D scale is a self-report measure of depression made up of 20 items that ask participants to report the frequency of various symptoms over the previous week using a four-category response scale (1 = *Rarely or none of the time [less than 1 day]*; 2 = *Some or a little of the time [1–2 days]*; 3 = *Occasionally or a moderate amount of time [3–4 days]*; 4 = *Most or all of the time [5–7 days]*). Four of the items require reverse-coding prior to analysis. After recoding, scores range from 0 to 60, with lower scores indicating lower levels of depression and higher scores indicating higher levels of depression. According to the original author of the scale, the stated intended use of the CES-D is as a screening instrument to identify individuals or groups who may be at risk for depression; scores greater than or equal to 16 indicate potential depression (Radloff, 1977). Details about the instrument and a downloadable version of the items are available at http://bit.ly/CES-D_inst. Table 1.3 shows the item stems. For analyses in this book, we use a recoded version of the ratings that range from 0 to 3.

The CES-D scale was selected as the example data for this book for several reasons. First, the CES-D scale was intended to function as a unidimensional measure of a single construct (depression; Radloff, 1977); as a result, it is well suited for analysis with unidimensional IRT models. Second, the CES-D items are in the public domain, and there are several real datasets available with responses to the items online (e.g., data from Donny et al., 2015). Third, this instrument includes a four-category ordinal response scale that is similar to those in many other surveys or questionnaires. Fourth, there have been numerous psychometric evaluations of the CES-D in published research (e.g., Cosco et al., 2020; González et al., 2017; Macêdo et al., 2018), but at the time of this writing, there have not been any published rating scale analyses of this instrument. Together, these characteristics make the CES-D scale a good candidate for an accessible and relevant demonstration of rating scale analysis using an IRT approach.

To facilitate the example analyses in this book, data from a recently published application of the CES-D scale were consulted. Specifically, the CES-D scale data used in the illustrations were collected as part of a larger study related to the impact of reduced-nicotine standards for

18

cigarettes among individuals who regularly smoked cigarettes (Donny et al., 2015). In this application, no details about the CES-D were reported related to rating scale analysis. The original data included responses from 839 participants who responded to the 20-item CES-D scale. The original data are publicly available for download from the National Institute on Drug Abuse data sharing website link for the Donny et al. study: https://datashare.nida.nih.gov/study/nidacenicp1s1. For data security purposes, the illustrations and examples are based on data that were simulated using the parameters obtained from an analysis of the CES-D responses at the baseline time point from Donny et al. (2015) with the generalized partial credit model (Muraki, 1997). Readers can download the simulated version of the CES-D data from the online supplement at **https://study.sagepub.com/researchmethods/qass/ wind-exploring-rating-scale-functioning** in order to complete the example analyses for this book.

Resources for Further Study

Readers who are new to IRT in general may find the following general introductory IRT texts helpful for learning about this approach in more detail:

DeAyala, R. J. (2009). *The theory and practice of item response theory.* The Guilford Press.

Embretson, S. E., & Reise, S. P. (2000). *Item response theory for psychologists.* Lawrence Erlbaum Associates, Publishers.

Hambleton, R. K., Swaminathan, H., & Rogers, H. J. (1991). *Fundamentals of item response theory* (Vol. 2). Sage.

Paek, I., & Cole, K. (2020). *Using R for item response theory model applications.* Routledge.

Readers who would like to learn more about IRT models for polytomous data may find the following texts helpful:

Nering, M. L., & Ostini, R. (Eds.). (2010). *Handbook of polytomous item response theory models.* Routledge.

Ostini, R., & Nering, M. L. (2005). *Polytomous item response theory models* (Vol. 144). Sage.

2 RASCH MODELS FOR RATING SCALE ANALYSIS

This chapter introduces and illustrates two popular measurement models that facilitate rating scale analysis: The Rating Scale model (RSM; Andrich, 1978) and the Partial Credit model (PCM; Masters, 1982), along with the Many-Facet Rasch model (MFRM; Linacre, 1989), which can be specified as an extension of both of these models. These models belong to the family of Rasch measurement theory models (Rasch, 1960; Wright & Mok, 2004), which is a useful framework for rating scale analysis (discussed further below).

Chapter 2 begins with a brief overview of Rasch measurement theory and Rasch models in general. Then, these models are introduced and illustrated using the example CES-D data. Chapter 3 provides a detailed illustration of rating scale analysis using the selected Rasch models.

What Is Rasch Measurement Theory?

Rasch measurement theory (Rasch, 1960) is a theoretical framework based on the premise that principles of measurement from the physical sciences should guide measurement procedures in the social and behavioral sciences. Georg Rasch proposed a theory for social and behavioral measurement that can be summarized in four requirements:

(1) The comparison between two stimuli should be independent of which particular individuals were instrumental for the comparison;

(2) and it should also be independent of which stimuli within the considered class were or might also have been compared.

(3) Symmetrically, a comparison between two individuals should be independent of which particular stimuli with the class considered were instrumental for the comparison;

(4) and it should also be independent of which other individuals were also compared on the same or on some other occasion.

(Rasch, 1961, pp. 331–332)

Together, these four requirements constitute *invariant measurement.* Rasch (1977) used the term *specific objectivity* to describe specific situations in which invariant measurement is approximated. Approximate

20

adherence to invariant measurement is considered a prerequisite for measurement in the context of Rasch measurement theory. In other words, from the perspective of Rasch measurement theory, it is not appropriate to interpret and use the results from measurement procedures unless there is evidence that the requirements for invariant measurement are appropriately satisfied.

The requirements for invariant measurement are related to two other requirements that characterize Rasch measurement theory. First, Rasch measurement theory requires that item responses adhere to *unidimensionality*. Unidimensionality occurs when one latent variable (i.e., construct) is sufficient to explain most of the variation in item responses. In the context of the CES-D measure of depression mentioned in Chapter 1, unidimensionality would imply that participants' level of depression is the primary variable that determines their responses. Second, Rasch measurement theory requires that item responses reflect *local independence*. Local independence occurs when participant responses to individual items are not statistically related to their responses to other items after controlling for the primary latent variable. In the CES-D scale, local independence implies that participants' responses to one item (e.g., Item 1: *I was bothered by things that usually don't bother me*) do not influence their responses to another item (e.g., Item 2: *I did not feel like eating; my appetite was poor*) beyond what could be predicted given their level of depression. One common cause of violations of local independence in survey research is item stems that contain the same or nearly the same statements. For example, researchers have observed violations of local independence in surveys that contain pairs of statements that are nearly identical but oriented in opposite directions. Using participant responses to the Interpersonal Reactivity Index measure of empathy, Yaghoubi Jami and Wind (2022) observed a violation of local independence between Item 16: *After seeing a play or movie, I have felt as though I were one of the characters* and Item 12, which is a reversed version of nearly the same statement: *Becoming extremely involved in a good book or movie is somewhat rare for me*. We will discuss methods that researchers can use to evaluate unidimensionality and local independence later in this chapter.

What Are Rasch Models?

Rasch models are measurement models that are theoretically and mathematically aligned with Rasch measurement theory (Rasch, 1960, see Chapter 1). Rasch models are mathematically similar to several other item response theory (IRT) models, such as the one-parameter logistic model (Birnbaum, 1968), but the theoretical perspective underlying the development and use of the model is different. Specifically, Rasch models serve as a guide for evaluating the characteristics of item response data; in other IRT approaches, models are selected whose parameters offer a good *representation* of the characteristics of the data. The major difference between the Rasch approach and other IRT models is that Rasch models use theory to evaluate the characteristics of item responses, whereas other IRT models use the characteristics of item responses to identify and select a model.

The simplest Rasch model is the dichotomous Rasch model for item responses (x) scored in two ordered categories ($x = 0, 1$). These responses are often observed in multiple-choice achievement tests or surveys where participants are asked to agree or disagree with statements. The dichotomous Rasch model states that the probability of Participant n scoring $x = 1$ rather than $x = 0$ on Item i is determined using the difference between the participant's location on the construct (e.g., the participant's level of depression) and the item's location on the construct (e.g., the level of depression required to agree with an item).

The equation for the dichotomous Rasch model appears in the literature in two formats that are mathematically equivalent but describe the model in slightly different terms: The exponent (exp) format, and the log-odds (ln) format. We will start with the log-odds format, which is visually simpler and clearly illustrates key characteristics of the theory underlying Rasch measurement:

$$\ln \left(\frac{P_{ni(x=1)}}{P_{ni(x=0)}} \right) = \theta_n - \delta_i, \tag{2.1}$$

In Equation 2.1, θ_n is the location of Participant n on the construct (i.e., person ability) and δ_i is the location of Item i on the construct (i.e., item difficulty).[1] In words, Equation 2.1 states that the log of the odds that Participant n provides a correct or positive response ($x = 1$), rather than an incorrect or negative response ($x = 0$) on Item i is determined by the difference between the participant location and the item location on the construct. When the difference between person

---

[1] In the original presentation of Rasch measurement theory, Rasch (1960) used the Greek letter "β" to represent person locations. In this text, the Greek letter "θ" is used for alignment with other recent publications on Rasch models and with the non-Rasch models that are presented in Chapter 4.

locations and item locations favors the person, this means that the person is more likely to score 1 than 0. In this case, item difficulty (i.e., the level of the construct required for a correct or positive response) is lower than the person's location on the latent variable (i.e., the person's level of the construct).

For example, in Figure 1.1, Participant B would be expected to provide a correct or positive response to Item 1 because the person location exceeds the item location. When the difference favors the item, this means that the person is more likely to score 0 than 1. In this case, the item difficulty exceeds the person's location. Participant A would be expected to provide an incorrect or negative response to Item 1 because the item location exceeds the person location.

Figure 2.1 illustrates this relationship using an item response function (IRF) for Item 1 and Item 2, both of which were scored in two categories ($x = 0, 1$). In the figure, the x-axis shows the latent variable, expressed as a logit (log-odds) scale. In many Rasch and IRT applications, logit scale estimates range from around −3 to 3 logits that reflect increasing levels of the latent variable as the logit scale progresses

Figure 2.1 Example Item Response Functions for the Dichotomous Rasch Model

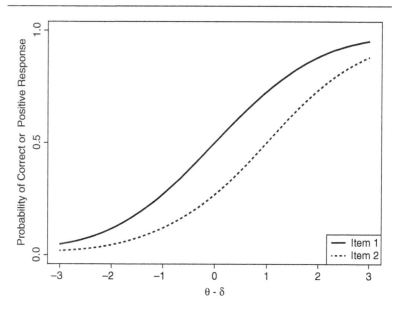

from low to high. The y-axis shows the conditional probability for a response in category 1 ($x = 1$). The lines show the expected pattern of response probabilities according to the dichotomous Rasch model for Item 1 (solid line) and Item 2 (dashed line). As participant locations on the construct increase (e.g., higher levels of depression), the probability for a positive rating ($x = 1$) also increases for both items.

The IRFs in Figure 2.1 reflect the requirements for invariant measurement, unidimensionality, and local independence as defined in Chapter 1 and earlier in this chapter because the difference between participant and item locations on the latent variable is sufficient to predict a response in category 1. In addition, for all locations on the x-axis, Item 1 is easier than Item 2, such that item ordering is invariant across participant locations on the latent variable.

It is also possible to state the dichotomous Rasch model equation using an exponent form such that the term on the left side of the equation is the *probability* for a response in category 1 rather than in category 0. This version of the model equation is mathematically equivalent to Equation 2.1, but it is presented differently. Specifically, log odds are transformed to probabilities.

The exponent format of the dichotomous Rasch model highlights the comparison between response categories. In the case of the dichotomous Rasch model, these categories are $x = 0$ and $x = 1$. The exponent format is useful for understanding Rasch models for rating scale data (discussed later in this chapter). The exponent form of the dichotomous Rasch model can be stated as:

$$\frac{P_{ni(x=1)}}{P_{ni(x=0)}} = \frac{\exp(\theta_n - \delta_i)}{1 + \exp(\theta_n - \delta_i)}. \tag{2.2}$$

In Equation 2.2, the parameters are defined the same way as they were in Equation 2.1.

Polytomous Rasch Models for Rating Scale Analysis

Building on the dichotomous Rasch model, researchers have proposed measurement models for data in three or more ordered categories (i.e., polytomous data), such as data that are obtained from attitude surveys or educational performance assessments. Polytomous Rasch models share the same basic requirements as the dichotomous Rasch model. However, unlike the dichotomous model, a score of $x = 1$ is *not* expected to become increasingly likely with increasing participant locations on the construct because scores in higher categories (e.g., $x = 2$ and $x = 3$) become more probable as participant locations on the construct increase. In the context of the CES-D scale, as participant depression increases, they are more likely to respond in a higher category.

Figure 2.2 illustrates this relationship for a rating scale with five ordered categories ($x = 0, 1, 2, 3, 4$). The x-axis shows the logit scale that represents the construct, and the y-axis shows the conditional probability for a rating in category k given participant and item locations. Separate lines show the conditional probabilities for each category in the rating scale. Moving from left to right on the x-axis, the probabilities for higher rating scale categories increase while the probabilities for lower rating scale categories decrease. In other words, as participant locations on the construct increase, they are more likely to respond in higher categories. This basic relationship can also be seen in Figure 2.3, which shows a polytomous IRF based on the rating scale category probabilities in Figure 2.2. In Figure 2.3, the y-axis shows the model-expected rating at each location on the logit scale, which is shown along the x-axis. As logit-scale locations increase, expected ratings increase.

Figure 2.2 Rating Scale Category Probability Curves

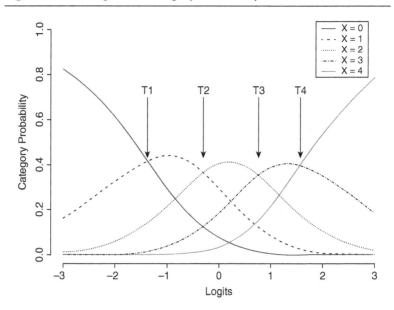

Figure 2.3 Expected Ratings

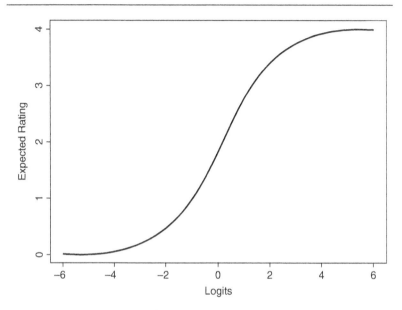

Why Are Polytomous Rasch Models Useful for Rating Scale Analysis?

Polytomous Rasch models are particularly suited to rating scale analysis for two main reasons. First, they are characterized by the same requirements as the dichotomous Rasch model. As a result, researchers can use polytomous Rasch models to evaluate item responses for evidence that they adhere to fundamental measurement properties. Discrepancies between model requirements and item responses alert researchers to components of a measurement procedure (e.g., items) that warrant revision, aspects of theory about the construct that may warrant reconsideration, and directions for future research.

Second, polytomous Rasch models model the probability for a rating in a given rating scale category using an *adjacent categories probability formulation.* This means that the model is based on comparisons between pairs of categories, as we saw in the exponent form of the dichotomous Rasch model (Equation 2.2), where the probability for $x = 1$ was compared to the probability for $x = 0$. The polytomous Rasch model equation can also be stated in exponent form, and it is nearly identical to the dichotomous version of the model (Equation 2.2) with two major differences. First, the polytomous Rasch model compares the probability for a response in category k (e.g., *Strongly Agree*) to the probability for a response in category $k - 1$ (e.g., *Agree*). Second, the equation includes a threshold parameter (τ) that represents the difficulty associated with a specific rating scale category. In Figure 2.2, thresholds are the intersection points between adjacent categories. We discuss thresholds in more detail later in this section.

The exponent form of the polytomous Rasch model is written as follows:

$$\frac{P_{ni(x=k)}}{P_{ni(x=k-1)} + P_{ni(x=k)}} = \frac{\exp[\theta_n - (\delta_i + \tau_k)]}{1 + \exp[\theta_n - (\delta_i + \tau_k)]}, \tag{2.3}$$

where θ_n and δ_i are defined as before. In Equation 2.3, the item difficulty parameter (δ) is combined with a *rating scale category threshold parameter* (τ_k). This means that we no longer consider items on their own, but we now consider items in combination with a set of ordered rating scale categories. As it is defined in many Rasch measurement theory applications (Andrich, 1978, 2013), the threshold parameter (τ) is the point on the logit scale at which the probability for a rating in category k is equal to the probability for a rating in category $k - 1$. For example, in the CES-D scale, the first threshold represents the level of depression at which participants are equally likely to respond in category 2 (*Some or a little of the time*) as they are to respond in category 1 (*Rarely or none of the time*).

For a rating scale with k categories, there are $k - 1$ threshold parameters. In Figure 2.2, there are four arrows that correspond to the thresholds between each category in a five-category rating scale. The comparison between adjacent categories (category k rather than category $k - 1$) is an important feature of polytomous Rasch models that distinguishes them from several other IRT models and facilitates analyses that are particularly useful for exploring the structure of rating scales. Specifically, this formulation allows analysts to identify disordered rating scale categories when they occur (e.g., Item 3 in Figure 1.3). Briefly, disordered categories occur when the level of the construct required to respond in each category does not match the intended order. For example, in the context of the CES-D scale, category disordering may occur if higher levels of depression are required to respond in category 4 (*Most or all of the time*) than are required to respond in category 3 (*Occasionally or a moderate amount of time*). We discuss category disordering further in the remaining chapters of this book. Several other popular polytomous IRT models, such as the Graded Response model (Samejima, 1969), use different probability formulations that do not allow analysts to use threshold estimates to identify category disordering when it occurs (discussed further in Chapters 4 and 6).

Rasch Models for Rating Scale Analysis

In practice, researchers conduct rating scale analysis with three types of Rasch models: The Rating Scale Model (RSM), the Partial Credit Model (PCM), and RSM and PCM formulations of the Many-Facet Rasch Model (MFRM). Table 1.2 provided an overview of these models in terms of the types of data and rating scale analysis goals that each of them accommodates.

Before we discuss the use of these models to examine specific indicators of rating scale analysis, it is helpful to understand the basic characteristics of each model and how they can be used to provide an overview of the psychometric quality of survey responses. Accordingly, the remainder of this chapter includes a description of each model followed by a short example analysis with the CES-D scale data (see Chapter 1). Relatively more detail is provided for the RSM because this model shares many characteristics in common with the other models in this chapter. Statistical software scripts for the analyses are provided in the online supplement at **https://study.sagepub.com/researchmethods/ qass/wind-exploring-rating-scale-functioning**. Chapter 3 provides a detailed demonstration of rating scale analyses using these models.

Rating Scale Model (RSM)

The RSM (Andrich, 1978), also known as the polytomous Rasch model, is a Rasch model for item responses in three or more ordered categories (e.g., $x = 0, 1, 2, ..., m$). As shown in Table 1.2, researchers use the RSM to analyze survey data when all of the items include the same set of response categories. The CES-D scale is an example of such an instrument because participants are presented with the same four rating scale categories for each item. In addition, researchers use the RSM to evaluate survey responses for evidence that they adhere to the fundamental measurement properties discussed in Chapter 1 and earlier in this chapter, including unidimensionality, local independence, and invariance. In the context of rating scale analysis, the RSM offers a relatively simple procedure that researchers can use to evaluate rating scale functioning for an overall set of items (discussed further in Chapter 3).

The RSM is an extension of the dichotomous Rasch model for polytomous data. In log-odds form, the RSM states that the log of the odds for a response in category k, rather than in category $k - 1$ is determined by the difference between the participant location (θ), item location (δ), and rating scale category threshold locations (τ) on the logit scale that represents the latent variable:

$$ln\left(\frac{P_{ni(x=k)}}{P_{ni(x=k-1)}}\right) = \theta_n - (\delta_i + \tau_k). \tag{2.4}$$

As we saw with the dichotomous Rasch model, the RSM can also be expressed by converting the log-odds form to an exponent form, which describes the probability for a rating in a given rating scale category (category x) as:

$$P_{ni(x=k)} = \frac{\exp \sum_{k=0}^{x} [\theta_n - (\delta_i + \tau_k)]}{\sum_{j=0}^{m} \sum_{k=0}^{j} [\theta_n - (\delta_i + \tau_k)]}. \tag{2.5}$$

For Participant n on Item i where the maximum category is m, the probability for a rating in category x is expressed as the sum of the probabilities for the steps up to category x divided by the sum of the probabilities for all of the steps in the rating scale.

The RSM provides analysts with estimates of participant, item, and rating scale category threshold locations on the latent variable. We will consider the information that the RSM provides using an illustrative analysis with the CES-D scale data.

Application of the RSM to the CES-D Scale Data

The RSM was used to analyze participant responses to the CES-D scale, which includes 20 items with a four-category response scale recoded to $x = 0, 1, 2, 3$ (see Chapter 1). Applying the RSM to the CES-D scale goes beyond total-score-level analyses of the instrument to provide information about individual participant, item, and rating scale category locations on an interval-level scale that represents the construct. In addition, the RSM provides information about the quality of item responses from the perspective of invariant measurement

(Rasch, 1960). Most relevant to this book, the initial application of the RSM to the CES-D scale data provides information that can be used to evaluate rating scale functioning.

For the current illustration, the RSM was applied using the Facets software (Linacre, 2020), which uses Joint Maximum Likelihood Estimation (JMLE). Briefly, JMLE is an iterative procedure that involves calculating estimates for the model parameters (θ, δ, τ) using observed item responses. The procedure converts the observed probabilities in the data to measures on a log-odds scale, alternating between calculating item estimates and person estimates to find estimates that reflect the observed responses. For additional details on JMLE and other estimation procedures for Rasch models and IRT models, please see DeAyala (2009). Following typical Rasch estimation procedures, the mean of the item locations was set to zero logits to provide a frame of reference for interpreting the parameter estimates on the logit scale.

Preliminary Analysis: Model-Data Fit

Before interpreting the parameter estimates from the RSM in detail, it is important to examine the results for evidence that the data approximately reflect the expectations of the model. The purpose of this *model-data fit* analysis is to ensure that it is reasonable and appropriate to interpret the results before proceeding with further analysis, including rating scale analyses. This kind of analysis can be considered along the lines of checking assumptions for statistical models, such as checking the normality assumption in regression analysis. However, in the Rasch framework, model-data fit analysis is related to a theoretical framework that reflects requirements for measurement. Specifically, the Rasch approach begins with the hypothesis that item responses fit the Rasch model, and the data are fit to the model as an initial step. Then, residuals, or discrepancies, between model estimates and the data, are examined for evidence of substantial deviations from model requirements.

There are numerous techniques that researchers use in practice to evaluate adherence to Rasch model requirements, and it is beyond the scope of this book to explore Rasch model fit analysis in great detail. In this chapter, we consider model-data fit for Rasch models using three indices that are relatively straightforward to interpret. In practice, researchers often use all three of these indices to provide a comprehensive overview of model-data fit before they proceed with interpreting the model results.

30

Rasch model-data fit indicators are calculated using *residuals*, which are numeric summaries of the degree to which the observed responses for each person on each item (i.e., the actual survey responses) match the responses that we would expect to see for each person-item combination if the parameter estimates (person locations, item locations, and threshold locations) were accurate. Residuals are calculated for each person-item combination as follows:

$$Y_{ni} = X_{ni} - E_{ni}, \tag{2.6}$$

where X_{ni} is the observed response for person n on item i, and E_{ni} is the model-expected response for person n on item i. Model-expected responses are calculated using person location estimates (θ), item difficulty estimates (δ), and threshold locations (τ). Residuals are positive when the observed response was higher than the expected response (e.g., a person responded *Strongly Agree* when the expected response was *Agree*). Residuals are negative when the observed response was lower than the expected response (e.g., a person responded *Agree* when the expected response was *Strongly Agree*). Larger values of Y_{ni} indicate that there was a large difference between the observed response and the response that the model expected for a given person-item combination, and smaller values of Y_{ni} indicate a small difference.

Researchers can use residuals to explore many aspects of model-data fit. In this chapter, we use them to calculate three model-data fit indices that are relatively straightforward to interpret: (1) proportion of variance explained by model estimates; (2) correlations among item-specific residuals; and (3) numeric summaries of model residuals for items and persons. Graphical analyses that are also relevant to evaluating model-data fit for the RSM are included in Chapter 3.

Unidimensionality: Proportion of Variance Explained by Model Estimates

To begin, researchers often examine model results for evidence of adherence to the Rasch model requirement of unidimensionality (see Chapter 1). One unidimensionality evaluation procedure that is aligned with the Rasch framework is to evaluate how much of the variation in participant responses can be attributed to a single latent variable, such as depression in the context of the CES-D scale. To evaluate this property in practice, researchers can calculate the proportion of variance in responses that can be explained using Rasch model estimates.

This procedure is conducted automatically in the Facets software program (Linacre, 2020). It can also be approximated using three components; the supplemental materials demonstrate how to calculate these components in the R software packages that support Rasch model analyses. First, the variance of the original responses (V_O) is calculated using observed responses (X_{ni} in Equation 2.6). Then, the variance of *residuals* (V_R) is calculated using the Y_{ni} values from Equation 2.6. These values are combined to find the proportion of response variance attributable to Rasch model estimates: $(V_O - V_R)/V_O$.

For the simulated CES-D data, the approximate proportion of variance explained by Rasch model estimates was 24.55%. This value is greater than the minimum value of 20% that Reckase (1979) recommended for Rasch model analyses of potentially multidimensional scales—providing support for the use of the RSM to analyze the CES-D data.

Local Independence: Correlations Among Item-Specific Residuals

Next, one can evaluate the Rasch model requirement of local independence by examining correlations between the residuals that are associated with each item. The idea behind this analysis is this: If items are locally independent (thus satisfying the model requirement), there should be *no* meaningful relationships among the responses to individual items after controlling for the primary latent variable. Low absolute values of inter-item residual correlations (e.g., $|r| \leq 0.30$) provide evidence to support local independence (Yen, 1984). For the example CES-D scale data, the absolute values of the inter-item residual correlations were all less than or equal to $|r| = 0.04$—thus providing support for the use of the RSM to analyze these item responses. Practically speaking, this means that participants' responses to each item did not affect their responses to the other items in the scale after controlling for their level of depression.

Item- and Person-Specific Fit Analysis

Perhaps one of the most useful features of Rasch models, including the RSM, is item- and person-specific fit analysis. Item- and person-fit indices help analysts identify *individual items* and *individual persons* whose response patterns do not match what would be expected if the item response data adhered to the model requirements. Such analyses can be useful from a diagnostic perspective to improve data quality (e.g., to identify items that may be candidates for removal prior to further analysis), to identify individual participants whose responses warrant additional exploration and consideration, to improve the quality of the instrument, to inform theory about the instrument or a sample, among other uses (see Chapter 1). In practice, many researchers use numeric summaries of item and person-specific residuals in the form of mean square error (MSE) statistics.

Specifically, one can examine unweighted or weighted means of standardized residuals for each item and person using outfit MSE statistics and infit MSE statistics, respectively (Smith, 2004). These statistics are calculated as follows. First, residuals are calculated for each item-person combination (Y_{ni}) using Equation 2.6. Then, standardized versions of the residuals (Z_{ni}) are calculated as:

$$Z_{ni} = Y_{ni} \big/ \sqrt{W_{ni}}, \tag{2.7}$$

where W_{ni} is the variance of X_{ni}, calculated as:

$$W_{ni} = \sum_{k=0}^{M_i} (k - E_{ni})^2 p_{nik}, \tag{2.8}$$

where p_{nik} is the probability for a response in Category k from Person n on Item i, and M_i is the maximum category for Item i.

Outfit MSE statistics are unweighted means of standardized residuals specific to individual items or persons, calculated as:

$$\text{Outfit MSE} = \sum_{n=1}^{N} z_{ni}{}^2 \big/ N. \tag{2.9}$$

Just as averages are sensitive to outliers in general statistical analyses, outfit MSE statistics are sensitive to extreme unexpected responses. In survey analyses, extreme unexpected responses occur when the observed response is much lower or higher than expected given model estimates. For example, an unexpected response could occur in the CES-D scale if a person with very mild or no depression responded *Most or All of the Time* on an item that would be considered a relatively strong indicator of depression. An unexpected response could also occur if a person with very severe depression responded *Rarely or None of the Time* to an item describing a common behavior among most of the participants, regardless of depression level.

Infit MSE statistics were developed to provide an indicator of model-data fit that is less sensitive to extreme residuals. These statistics are calculated in a similar manner as outfit MSE, but they are weighted by response variance (W_{ni}):

$$\text{Infit MSE} \; = \; \sum_{n=1}^{N} W_{ni}Z_{ni}{}^2 \bigg/ \sum_{n=1}^{N} W_{ni}. \qquad (2.10)$$

Because they are weighted, infit MSE statistics are less sensitive to extreme unexpected responses.

It is beyond the scope of the current text to discuss the interpretation of outfit and infit MSE in great detail; however, some basic guidance will be provided here. In contrast to some other statistics such as t-statistics, which have known distributions for specific sample sizes, there is no known sampling distribution for outfit and infit MSE statistics. As a result, they cannot be directly evaluated for statistical significance. Instead, many researchers use critical values (i.e., cut scores) based on practical guidance and empirical methods (e.g., bootstrap methods) to evaluate them in practical applications (DeAyala, 2009; Seol, 2016; Walker et al., 2018; Wolfe, 2013). In general, many researchers agree that values of outfit and infit MSE around 1.00 indicate acceptable fit to a Rasch model (Smith, 2004; Wu & Adams, 2013). Values that exceed 1.00 indicate more variation than expected in the responses associated with an item or person, and values that are less than 1.00 indicate less variation than expected. In many practical applications, researchers consider values of outfit and infit MSE that substantially exceed 1.00 as more cause for concern compared to low values of outfit and infit MSE (Linacre & Wright, 1994). When items or persons have notably high outfit and/or infit MSE statistics, analysts can examine the responses associated with the individual item or person in more detail for potential explanations. In some cases, it may be prudent to remove extreme misfitting items or persons from the data and reestimate model parameters in order to ensure meaningful interpretation of model results.

For the CES-D scale data, the mean outfit and infit MSE fit statistics were close to 1.00 for items (outfit MSE: M = 0.99, infit MSE: M = 1.01) and persons (outfit MSE = 0.99, infit MSE: M = 1.00). For items, the outfit MSE statistics ranged from 0.75 for Item 5 (*I had trouble keeping my mind on what I was doing*), which had responses that had the least amount of variation compared to model expectations, to 1.24 for Item 17 (*I had crying spells*), which had the most-frequent unexpected responses compared to model expectations. Infit MSE statistics ranged

34

from 0.73 for Item 5 to 1.34 for Item 17 (*I had crying spells*). Figure 2.4 illustrates the distribution of item fit statistics from the RSM. Person-fit statistics are summarized visually in Figure 2.5. Person-infit MSE ranged from 0.36 for the participant with the most deterministic (i.e., predicable) response to 2.54 for the participant with the most frequent and substantial unexpected responses. Likewise, outfit MSE ranged from 0.37 to 1.98. Examination of the histograms of person-fit statistics suggests that the MSE fit statistics were around 1.00 for the majority of the sample. Although it is possible to explore item fit and person fit in more detail, these preliminary results are sufficient to proceed with further psychometric analyses with the RSM, including rating scale analysis.

Overall RSM Results

Figure 2.6 summarizes the results from the RSM analysis of the CES-D scale data using a Wright Map (i.e., a "variable map" or "item-person map"; see Wilson, 2011), which is a visual display that depicts the estimated locations for persons and items on a single linear scale that represents the construct. Wright maps are a key feature of Rasch measurement theory because they provide a concise summary of model results that capitalizes on the key strengths of Rasch models (Engelhard & Wang, 2020). Specifically, these displays illustrate the locations of individual items, persons, and rating scale categories on a single continuum that represents the construct (e.g., depression). As a result, they allow analysts to quickly visualize the location of individual elements within each facet (e.g., individual persons and items), the overall shape of the distributions of these elements, and to make comparisons between facet locations on the same scale. This visual summary of model estimates is invaluable for understanding and communicating the results from Rasch model analyses.

The first column in the Wright map (labeled "Logit") for the RS analysis of the CES-D scale shows the log-odds scale. This is the metric on which person, item, and rating scale category threshold locations were estimated. Low values indicate less-severe depression and high values indicate more-severe depression. The second column shows the distribution of person locations on the logit scale, where an asterisk symbol (*) represents 9 people and a period symbol (.) represents between 1 and 8 people. For persons, relatively low locations on the logit scale indicate persons with relatively mild depressive symptoms,

Figure 2.4 Histograms of Item Fit Statistics for the Rating Scale Model

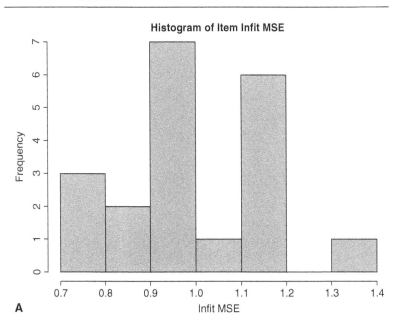

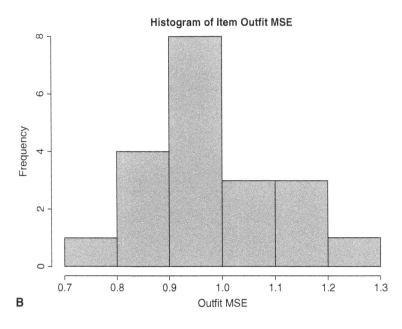

Figure 2.5 Histograms of Person-Fit Statistics for the Rating Scale Model

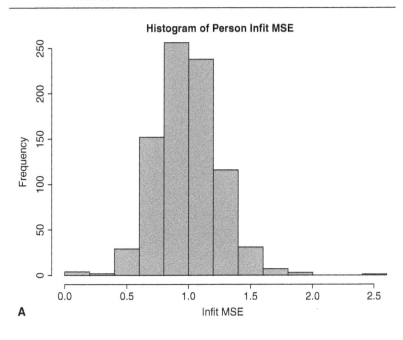

A

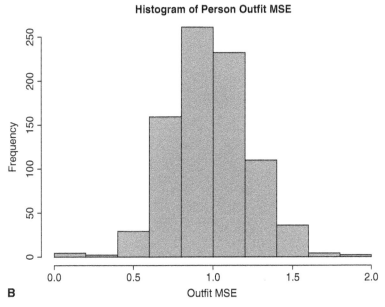

B

Figure 2.6 Wright Map for the CES-D Scale Data Based on the RSM
Note: In the Logit column, numbers indicate values on the log-odds scale. In the Person column, asterisks (*) indicate 9 people and periods (.) indicate between 1 and 8 people. In the Item column, numbers indicate item numbers from the CES-D scale. In the Scale column, numbers indicate category numbers from the recoded CES-D scale, which ranges from 0 to 3. Dashed horizontal lines indicate thresholds between adjacent categories in the scale

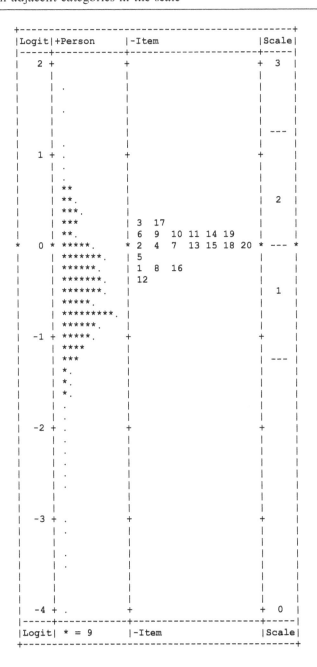

38

and relatively high locations on the logit scale indicate persons with relatively severe depressive symptoms. These results indicate that the average person location was equal to -0.54 logits, and that the distribution of person locations was approximately normal or bell-shaped.

The third column of Figure 2.6 shows the locations of the overall item estimates (δ) based on the RSM, with item numbers used to mark estimated item locations. For items, low locations on the logit scale indicate that an item requires participants to experience relatively mild depressive symptoms to report that they frequently experience or perform the stated behavior, and high locations on the logit scale indicate that an item requires participants to experience relatively severe depressive symptoms to report that they frequently experience or perform the stated behavior. In the estimation procedure, the average item location was set to zero logits to provide a frame of reference for interpreting the logit scale. The results from this analysis indicate that on average, the persons had lower locations on the logit scale relative to items—indicating that the participants exhibited relatively low levels of depression.

The final column of Figure 2.6 shows the estimated locations for the rating scale category thresholds using dashed horizontal lines between numeric labels for the category numbers ($x = 0, 1, 2, 3$). Because the CES-D rating scale includes four categories, there are three rating scale category threshold estimates (τ_1, τ_2, τ_3). The estimated threshold locations in logits were as follows: $\tau_1 = -0.30$, $\tau_2 = -0.25$, and $\tau_3 = 0.55$. The distance between the first and second thresholds (τ_1 and τ_2) is very small (approximately 0.05 logits). To further illustrate these results, Figure 2.7 shows rating scale category probability curves for the CES-D rating scale, as estimated with the RSM. Both the numeric and graphical results indicate that the second rating scale category does not have a distinct range on the logit scale at which it is the most probable. We consider these results in more detail in Chapter 3.

Partial Credit Model (PCM)

The PCM (Masters, 1982) is similar in many ways to the RSM: It is a polytomous Rasch model for item responses in three or more ordered categories (e.g., $x = 0, 1, 2, \ldots, m$) that provides researchers with estimates of person locations (θ), item locations (δ), and rating scale category threshold locations (τ) on a linear scale that represents a latent variable. The major difference from the RSM is that in the PCM,

Figure 2.7 Rating Scale Category Probability Curves for the CES-D Scale Data Based on the RSM

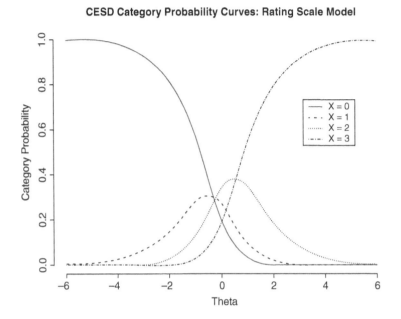

threshold locations are calculated separately for each item. As shown in Table 1.2, this feature allows researchers to use the PCM when items have different response scales, and when they want to evaluate rating scale functioning separately for each item. We discuss choosing between the RSM and PCM in more detail in Chapters 3 and 6.

In log-odds form, the PCM states that the log of the odds that Participant n gives a rating in Category k rather than in category $k-1$ is determined by the difference between the Participant's location on the construct (θ) and the combination of the item location parameter (δ_i) with the threshold parameter (τ_k), specific to Item i:

$$\ln\left(\frac{P_{ni(x=k)}}{P_{ni(x=k-1)}}\right) = \theta_n - \delta_{ik} \qquad (2.11)$$

In exponent form, the PCM expresses the probability for a rating in a given rating scale category (category x) is stated as:

$$P_{ni(x=k)} = \frac{\exp \sum_{k=0}^{x} (\theta_n - \delta_{ik})}{\sum_{j=0}^{m} \sum_{k=0}^{j} (\theta_n - \delta_{ik})}. \tag{2.12}$$

In the PCM, the item location parameter (δ_i) is combined with the threshold parameter (τ_k) for each item such that δ_{ik} is the location on the logit scale at which there is an equal probability for a rating in category k and category $k - 1$, specific to item i. This means that each item has its own unique set of threshold estimates, as illustrated in Figure 1.3.

When the PCM is applied to item response data, it provides estimates of participant, item, and rating scale category threshold locations specific to each item. These results can be used to examine a variety of psychometric properties, including rating scale functioning. The PCM is particularly useful for rating scale analysis because it facilitates an examination of rating scale functioning specific to each item in a scale. This information can be useful for identifying individual items for which rating scales are not functioning as expected. Chapter 3 provides a more in-depth exploration of the use of the PCM for this purpose.

Application of the PCM to the CES-D Data

The PCM was used to analyze participant responses to the CES-D scale using the Facets software with item locations centered at zero logits. As noted in the demonstration of the RSM, it is important to evaluate the degree to which item responses approximate Rasch model requirements before interpreting parameter estimates in detail. The model-data fit analysis results for the PCM were similar to those reported earlier for the RSM. Specifically, the PCM estimates explained 25.2% of the variance in observed responses and all of the inter-item residual correlations had absolute values equal to or less than or equal to $|r| = 0.03$. For items, the largest values of outfit MSE and infit MSE were observed for the recoded version of Item 12 (*I was happy*; outfit MSE = 1.26; infit MSE = 1.22) and the recoded version of Item 16 (*I enjoyed life*; outfit MSE = 1.24; infit MSE = 1.19). The lowest values of the MSE statistics were observed for Item 5 (*I had trouble keeping my mind on what I was doing*; outfit MSE = 0.88; infit MSE = 0.89).

Overall, the results from the PCM analysis of the CES-D scale data are similar to those from the RSM. Figure 2.8 summarizes the results using a Wright Map in the same format as presented in Figure 2.6 for the RSM. The major difference is that the rating scale category thresholds are estimated separately for each item; these item-specific thresholds are shown in the 20 columns to the right of the overall item locations. The thresholds that correspond to each item are presented in a column labeled "S" for *scale* followed by the item number. Examination of the threshold estimates indicates that there are differences in the structure of the rating scale across the CES-D items. We explore these differences in detail using rating scale category probability curves and other indicators in Chapter 3.

Extending the Rating Scale and Partial Credit Models: The Many-Facet Rasch Model (MFRM)

In many assessment contexts, additional components of the assessment system besides persons and items contribute to item responses in important ways. Linacre (1989) proposed the Many-Facet Rasch Model (MFRM) as a flexible extension of Rasch models that allows researchers to include explanatory variables ("facets"). The MFRM is similar to a logistic regression model where researchers can examine the relationship between an independent and dependent variable controlling for other variables.

The MFRM was originally proposed in the context of performance assessments in which raters (i.e., judges) score participant performances. In this context, raters can be included as a facet to estimate rater severity levels in the same frame of reference as participants and items. This model also allows researchers to examine the impact of differences in rater severity on the estimates of student achievement, item difficulty, and rating scale category thresholds. Beyond rater-mediated assessments, the MFRM can be applied to a variety of contexts in which it is useful to include additional explanatory facets besides item and person locations. For example, many researchers use MFRMs to estimate logit-scale locations related to item or person features, such as demographic subgroups of persons, item types, or administrations of an assessment procedure in longitudinal designs (e.g., Gordon et al., 2021; Ho, 2019; Primi et al., 2019; Toffoli et al., 2016).

The MFRM is a flexible model that can be used to extend each of the Rasch models that have been discussed so far in this book (dichotomous, RSM, and PCM). The MFRM can also be used to extend Rasch models that are not described in this book, including the binomial trials

Figure 2.8 Wright Map for the CES-D Scale Data Based on the PCM

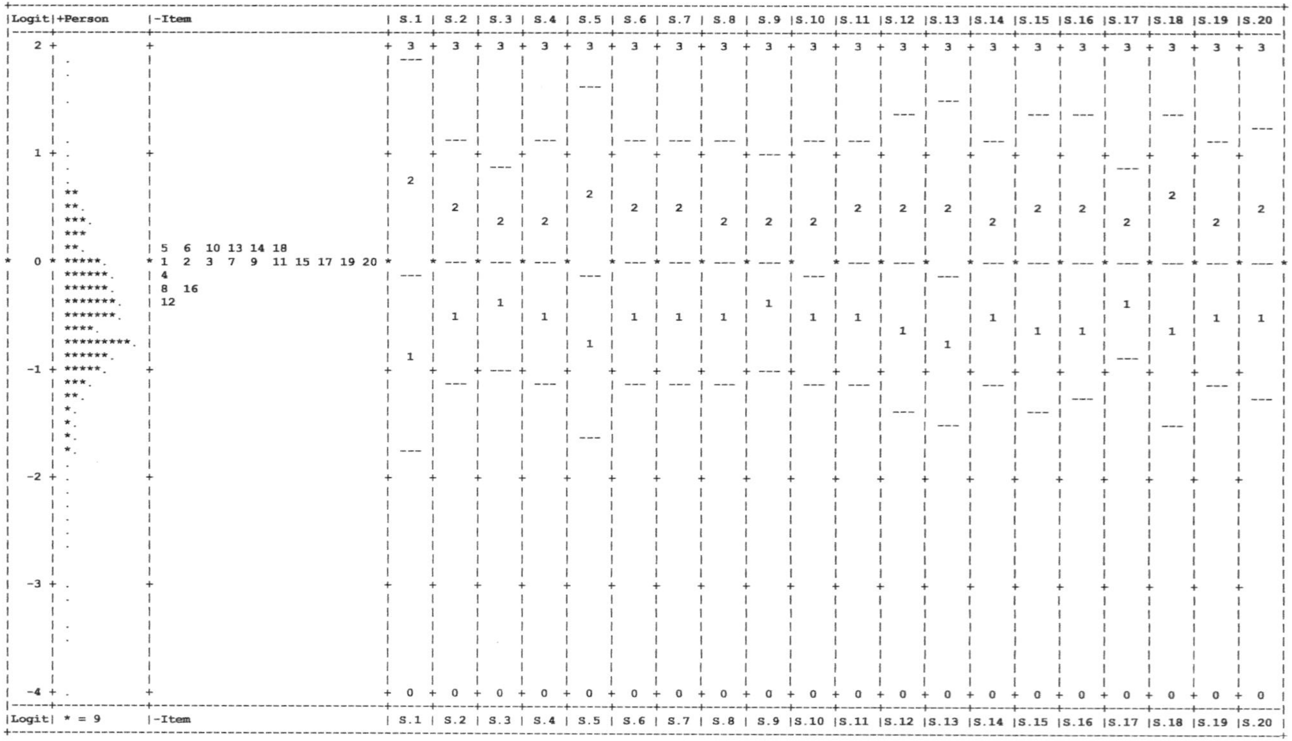

Note: See the note for Figure 2.6 for descriptions of the Logit, Person, and Item columns. Separate scale columns are presented for each item, labeled "S." followed by the item number from the CES-D scale

and the Poisson counts Rasch models (see Wright & Mok, 2004). Given its flexible nature, there is no single formulation of the MFRM that appears in the literature. Instead, researchers specify their own unique set of facets and add them to an appropriate Rasch model to reflect their measurement context. As shown in Table 1.2, this feature allows researchers to use the MFRM to examine rating scale functioning related to explanatory variables that are unique to each assessment context. We discuss this use of the MFRM in Chapter 3.

In the context of rating scale analysis, the MFRM can be used to extend the RSM and the PCM. A general form of a Rating Scale model formulation of the MFRM (RS-MFRM) can be stated in log-odds form as:

$$\ln\left(\frac{P_{n(x=k)}}{P_{n(x=k-1)}}\right) = \theta_n - \sum_{\text{facets}} \varepsilon - \tau_k, \tag{2.13}$$

where θ_n and τ_k are defined as in the RSM and $\sum_{\text{facets}} \varepsilon$ is a linear combination of the researcher-specified facets that reflect aspects of the assessment system. The estimate of the person's location on the latent variable (θ_n) is controlled (i.e., adjusted) for the facets included in $\sum_{\text{facets}} \varepsilon$. For example, a researcher might specify a RS-MFRM that includes facets for participants, items, and participant education-level subgroups. This allows the analyst to examine the probability for a response controlling for differences related to participant education level. Stated in log-odds form, this RS-MFRM is:

$$\ln\left(\frac{P_{nji(x=k)}}{P_{nji(x=k-1)}}\right) = \theta_n - \gamma_j - \delta_i - \tau_k, \tag{2.14}$$

where θ_n, δ_i, and τ_k are defined as in the RSM, and γ_j is the logit-scale location for participant subgroup (e.g., education level) j. Researchers may use the RS-MFRM when they want to examine rating scale functioning for an overall set of items while controlling for an explanatory facet such as education level (see Table 1.2).

Similarly, a PCM formulation of the MFRM (PC-MFRM) with the same facets could be specified as:

$$\ln\left(\frac{P_{nji(x=k)}}{P_{nji(x=k-1)}}\right) = \theta_n - \gamma_j - \delta_i - \tau_{ik}, \tag{2.15}$$

In the PC-MFRM, the threshold parameter includes subscripts for items and rating scale categories (τ_{ik})—indicating that separate rating scale category thresholds are estimated for each item in the same manner as was presented for the PCM. This would allow researchers to examine rating scale functioning for individual items while controlling for an explanatory facet such as education level.

The PC-MFRM can also be specified to allow researchers to examine rating scale functioning specific to the levels of an explanatory facet. For example, researchers may wish to evaluate the degree to which a rating scale functions in a comparable way between participants with different levels of education. This type of model could be specified by changing the subscript on the threshold parameter so that thresholds vary across the j education level subgroups:

$$\ln\left(\frac{P_{nji(x=k)}}{P_{nji(x=k-1)}}\right) = \theta_n - \gamma_j - \delta_i - \tau_{jk}, \qquad (2.16)$$

In this specification, the threshold parameter includes subscripts for participant subgroups and rating scale categories (τ_{jk})—indicating that separate rating scale category thresholds are estimated for each subgroup. In practice, the PC-MFRM is particularly useful for rating scale analysis because it facilitates an examination of rating scale functioning specific to each level of a facet of interest in an assessment system (see Table 1.2). This information can be useful for identifying individual levels of facets for which rating scales are not functioning as expected, and to examine the consistency of rating scale functioning across levels of facets (e.g., across participant subgroups). Chapter 3 provides a more in-depth exploration of the use of the PC-MFRM for this purpose.

Application of the PC-MFRM to the CES-D Data

Next, we will apply the PC-MFRM given in Equation 2.16 to analyze participant responses to the CES-D scale. In the CES-D scale data examined in this book, participants' education level was reported using six categories: (1) eighth grade or less, (2) some high school, (3) high school or high-school graduate equivalent, (4) completed some college or two-year degree, (5) completed four-year degree, and (6) graduate or professional degree. As in the previous analyses presented in this chapter, the mean of the item locations was set to zero logits.

In addition, the logit scale location for the eighth grade or less education level subgroup was fixed to zero logits, and the remaining education level subgroup locations were estimated freely. This provided a frame of reference for interpreting and comparing participant subgroups on the logit scale.

As noted earlier in the demonstration of the RSM and the PCM, it is important to evaluate the degree to which item responses approximate Rasch model requirements before interpreting parameter estimates in detail. For the PC-MFRM, the fit analysis results generally agreed with those from the RSM and PCM analyses. Specifically, PC-MFRM estimates explained 24.55% of the variance in observed responses, and the absolute value of each of the inter-item residual correlations was less than or equal to $|r| = 0.04$.

Figure 2.9 summarizes the results using a Wright Map in the same format as presented earlier for the RSM and the PCM, with an additional column (the third column) that shows the logit scale locations for each education-level subgroup. In addition, rating scale category thresholds are estimated separately for each subgroup; these subgroup-specific thresholds are shown in the six columns to the right of the overall item locations. The thresholds that correspond to each item are presented in a column labeled "S" for *scale* followed by the subgroup number. Examination of the threshold estimates indicates that there are differences in the structure of the rating scale across the CES-D items. We explore these differences using rating scale category probability curves and other indicators specific to each education subgroup in detail in Chapter 3.

Chapter Summary

This chapter began with a brief overview of Rasch measurement theory as a framework characterized by clear requirements that reflect measurement properties in the physical sciences. Then, two popular Rasch models for rating scale analysis were introduced with example applications using the CES-D data: The Rating Scale Model (RSM; Andrich, 1978) and the Partial Credit Model (PCM; Masters, 1982). Both of these models provide estimates of person locations, item locations, and rating scale threshold locations on a linear scale that represents a latent variable. The major difference between the models is that the PCM specifies rating scale thresholds separately for each item. Researchers may choose the RSM when they want an overall summary of rating scale functioning without item-specific details. Researchers may choose the PCM when they want item-specific details about rating scale functioning (see Table 1.2, discussed in more detail in Chapters 3

Figure 2.9 Wright Map for the CES-D Scale Data Based on the PC-MFRM

Note: See the note for Figure 2.6 for descriptions of the Logit, Person, and Item columns. In the Education Subgroup column, numbers indicate subgroups of participants with different levels of education: (1) eighth grade or less, (2) some high school, (3) high school or high school graduate equivalent, (4) completed some college or two-year degree, (5) completed four-year degree, and (6) graduate or professional degree. Separate scale columns are presented for each Education Subgroup, labeled "S." followed by the subgroup number as indicated in the Education Subgroup column

```
+--------------------------------------------------------------------------------------------+
|Logit|+Person   |+Education Subgroup|-Item                       | S.1 | S.2 | S.3 | S.4 | S.5 | S.6 |
|-----+----------+------------------+--------------------------+-----+-----+-----+-----+-----+-----|
|  2 +          +                  +                          + 3  +  3  +  3  +  3  +  3  +  3  |
|    | .        |                  |                          |    |     |     |     |     |     |
|    | .        |                  |                          |    |     |     |     |     |     |
|    | .        |                  |                          |    |     |     |     |     |     |
|    | .        |                  |                          |    |     |     |     |     |     |
|    | .        |                  |                          |    | --- | --- | --- | --- | --- |
|  1 + .        +                  +                          +    +     +     +     +     +     |
|    | *.       |                  |                          |    |     |     |     |     |     |
|    | **.      |                  |                          | 2  |  2  |  2  |  2  |  2  |  2  |
|    | **.      |                  |                          |    |     |     |     |     |     |
|    | ***.     |                  | 3   17                   |    |     |     |     |     |     |
|    | **.      | 2 6              | 6   9   10 11 14 19      |    |     |     |     |     |     |
*  0 * ****.    * 1 3 4 5          * 2   4   7   13 15 18 20 * --- *     *     *     *     *     |
|    | ****.    |                  | 5                        |    | --- |     |     |     |     |
|    | ******.  |                  | 1   8   16               |    |     |     |     |     |     |
|    | ******.  |                  | 12                       |    |     |     |     |     |     |
|    | ********  |                  |                          | 1  |  1  |  1  |  1  |  1  |  1  |
|    | *****.   |                  |                          |    |     |     |     |     |     |
|    | *****.   |                  |                          |    |     |     |     |     |     |
|    | *********. |                |                          |    |     |     |     |     |     |
| -1 + ******.  +                  +                          +    +     +     +     +     +     |
|    | ***.     |                  |                          |    | --- |     |     |     |     |
|    | ***.     |                  |                          |    |     | --- | --- | --- | --- |
|    | ***.     |                  |                          |    |     |     |     |     |     |
|    | *.       |                  |                          |    |     |     |     |     |     |
|    | *.       |                  |                          |    |     |     |     |     |     |
|    | *        |                  |                          |    |     |     |     |     |     |
|    | *.       |                  |                          |    |     |     |     |     |     |
| -2 + .        +                  +                          +    +     +     +     +     +     |
|    | .        |                  |                          |    |     |     |     |     |     |
|    | .        |                  |                          |    |     |     |     |     |     |
|    | .        |                  |                          |    |     |     |     |     |     |
|    | .        |                  |                          |    |     |     |     |     |     |
|    | .        |                  |                          |    |     |     |     |     |     |
|    | .        |                  |                          |    |     |     |     |     |     |
| -3 +          +                  +                          +    +     +     +     +     +     |
|    | .        |                  |                          |    |     |     |     |     |     |
|    | .        |                  |                          |    |     |     |     |     |     |
|    |          |                  |                          |    |     |     |     |     |     |
|    |          |                  |                          |    |     |     |     |     |     |
|    |          |                  |                          |    |     |     |     |     |     |
| -4 + .        +                  +                          + 0  +  0  +  0  +  0  +  0  +  0  |
|-----+----------+------------------+--------------------------+-----+-----+-----+-----+-----+-----|
|Logit| * = 9    |+Education Subgroup|-Item                    | S.1 | S.2 | S.3 | S.4 | S.5 | S.6 |
+--------------------------------------------------------------------------------------------+
```

and 6). Next, the Many-Facet Rasch Model (MFRM; Linacre, 1989) was presented and illustrated with the CES-D data as an extension of Rasch models that can be customized to reflect a variety of contexts and data analysis purposes that are relevant for rating scale analysis. Building on this content, Chapter 3 presents and illustrates techniques for exploring rating scale functioning using polytomous Rasch models.

3 ILLUSTRATION OF RATING SCALE ANALYSIS WITH POLYTOMOUS RASCH MODELS

Chapter 3 illustrates rating scale analysis using the models presented in Chapter 2: The Rating Scale model (RSM), the Partial Credit model (PCM), and the PCM formulation of the Many Facet Rasch Model (PC-MFRM). Recall from Chapter 2 that these models are appropriate for item responses in three or more ordered categories, and that they facilitate a variety of goals related to rating scale analysis (see Tables 1.2 and 3.1). Using analyses of the CES-D scale data with the RSM as an example, the chapter begins with an overview of rating scale analysis indices that are available with polytomous Rasch measurement theory models. Then, applications with the PCM and PC-MFRM are presented and discussed, with an emphasis on how these models are different from the RSM and when they may be preferred. Statistical software scripts are provided in the online supplement at **https://study.sagepub.com/research methods/qass/wind-exploring-rating-scale-functioning** that correspond to the analyses in this chapter.

Several researchers (Engelhard & Wind, 2013, 2018; Linacre, 2002; Wright & Masters, 1982) have demonstrated how polytomous Rasch measurement theory models, including the RSM, PCM, and various specifications of the MFRM, can facilitate rating scale analyses. The indicators included in this chapter provide information about rating scale functioning that is relevant for many practical purposes during scale development, evaluation, and interpretation. Readers can consult the original presentations of these methods for additional technical details about the development of the selected indices as well as other indices that may be useful in some cases.

In this book, rating scale analysis indicators are grouped into three major categories: (1) *category ordering* indices; (2) *category precision* indices; and (3) *category comparability* indices. Table 3.1 provides an overview of these indices as they relate to the polytomous Rasch models discussed in this chapter. The contents of this table are elaborated and illustrated in the remainder of the chapter.

Rating Scale Analysis With the Rating Scale Model

The RSM facilitates rating scale analysis for rating scales where all of the items have the same response scale (see Table 1.2). In addition to the general reasons for using Rasch models related to evaluating

Table 3.1 Overview of Rating Scale Category Functioning Indices Based on Polytomous Rasch Models

Groups of Indices	Guiding Question	RSM	PCM	PC-MFRM
Rating scale category ordering	To what extent do higher rating scale categories indicate higher locations on the construct?	One set of ordering indices for all items	Ordering indices specific to individual items	Ordering indices specific to levels of explanatory facets
Rating scale category precision	To what extent do individual rating scale categories reflect distinct ranges on the construct?	One set of precision indices for all items	Precision indices specific to individual items	Precision indices specific to levels of explanatory facets
Rating Scale Category Comparability	To what extent do rating scale categories have a similar interpretation and use across assessment components or subgroups of participants?	N/A	Comparability across items	Comparability across levels of explanatory facets

item responses for evidence of fundamental measurement properties, researchers also use the RSM when they want an overall picture of rating scale functioning without distinguishing between individual items. In addition, some researchers use the RSM to evaluate rating scale functioning after they first apply the PCM and determine that the scale structure is relatively comparable across items. In this case, details about rating scale functioning for individual items may not be needed. In this section, we will consider how analysts can use information from

50

the RSM to evaluate rating scales for evidence of category ordering and category precision.

Rating Scale Category Ordering

Rating scale category ordering means that there is evidence that the *intended* ordering of the rating scale categories (e.g., *Rarely or none of the time* < *Some or a little of the time* < *Occasionally or a moderate amount of time* < *Most or all of the time*) matches the *empirical* ordering of those rating scale categories on the construct, as estimated using a polytomous Rasch model. In other words, rating scale category ordering means that categories that are higher in the ordinal rating scale require participants to have higher locations on the construct compared to lower categories. When this occurs, higher ratings correspond to higher locations on the construct. These indices are important because they provide evidence that participant responses can be interpreted in the intended direction. For example, in the CES-D scale, rating scale category ordering means that the rating scale categories reflect increasing levels of depression as they progress from *Rarely or none of the time* to *Most or all of the time*. Evidence of intended rating scale category ordering allows analysts to interpret and use ratings in successive categories as evidence of higher levels of depression.

Examining rating scale category ordering is particularly important in measurement applications that include neutral rating scale categories. In these contexts, rating scale ordering indicators can help analysts understand whether their participants are using the neutral category in the intended order relative to the other categories, if the category may need to be combined with an adjacent category, and if the category may warrant reconsideration or removal in future administrations of the instrument.

Polytomous Rasch models provide three major tools with which researchers can evaluate rating scale category ordering: Average participant locations (theta (θ) estimates) within rating scale categories, location estimates of rating scale category thresholds (τ), and the order of category probability curves. Researchers can use these indices as evidence that participants' empirical use of rating scale categories reflects the hypothesized order of the categories, given the ordinal rating scale.

Average Participant Locations Within Rating Scale Categories

One tool for evaluating rating scale category ordering is to examine the average location estimates on the theta scale (θ) for participants who provided responses within each category. If rating scale categories are ordered as expected, participants with higher locations on the logit scale should provide responses in higher categories more often, and vice versa. For example, in the CES-D scale, participants who respond in higher rating scale categories would be expected to have higher levels of depression compared to participants who respond in lower rating scale categories.

In practice, researchers can use polytomous Rasch models to estimate participant locations (θ), and then examine the average location for participants who responded in each category using numeric estimates. This information can help researchers understand whether participants who respond in different categories of the rating scale have distinct locations on the construct, and if these differences are in the expected order.

Table 3.2 shows the average participant location estimates from the RSM for participants who responded in each category of the CES-D rating scale. The average estimates increased monotonically (i.e., they did not decrease) as the categories progress from low ($x = 0$: $M_\theta = -1.10$) to high ($x = 3$; $M_\theta = -0.14$). This result suggests that the categories in the CES-D rating scale correspond to higher locations on the latent variable of depression. In other words, the rating scale categories were oriented as expected: Participants who responded in higher categories tended to have higher levels of depression.

Logit-Scale Location Estimates of Rating Scale Category Thresholds

Another technique for evaluating rating scale category ordering with polytomous Rasch models is to examine the estimated locations for

Table 3.2 Rating Scale Category Calibrations From the RSM

Rating Scale Category	% of Ratings	Average Participant Location Estimate (θ)	Threshold Location		Absolute Distance Between Adjacent Threshold Estimates
			Threshold Estimate (τ)	Standard Error	
0	47%	−1.10	N/A	N/A	N/A
1	26%	−0.73	−0.30	0.02	N/A
2	19%	−0.40	−0.26	0.02	0.04
3	8%	−0.14	0.55	0.03	0.81

each rating scale category threshold (τ_k) for evidence that the observed order matches the expected order. For example, recall that the CES-D scale has four rating scale categories ($x = 0$: *Rarely or none of the time;* $x = 1$: *Some or a little of the time;* $x = 2$: *Occasionally or a moderate amount of time;* $x = 3$: *Most or all of the time*). For this four-category scale, there are three thresholds (τ_1, τ_2, τ_3). If the categories are ordered as expected, the threshold estimates should be ordered such that $\tau_1 < \tau_2$ and $\tau_2 < \tau_3$. Adherence to this expected order implies that each successive rating scale category requires participants to have higher levels of depression. Researchers can examine the empirical order of threshold estimates on the logit scale to evaluate rating scale category ordering.

Linacre (2002) noted that rating scale category threshold disordering "indicates that a category represents too narrow a segment on the latent variable or a concept that is poorly defined in the minds of the respondents" (p. 114). This disordering can occur for several reasons. For example, disordering may occur when there are infrequent observations in the higher category associated with the threshold. For example, in a four-category rating scale ($x = 0, 1, 2, 3$), the second and third thresholds (τ_2 and τ_3) could sometimes be disordered if there were relatively few observations in the highest category ($x = 3$) compared to the third category ($x = 2$). We will see an example of such disordering for Item 11 in the CES-D scale with the PCM analysis later in this chapter. Accordingly, researchers can also examine the frequency or percentage of ratings in each category to further understand threshold ordering and disordering in their data.

Threshold disordering can also occur when participants with higher measures more readily select the lower category associated with the threshold. For example, in a four-category rating scale, the second and third thresholds could sometimes be disordered if the participants who tended to respond in the second category ($x = 2$) had *higher* locations on the theta scale (e.g., more-severe levels of depression) compared to the participants who tended to respond in the third category ($x = 3$).

In other cases, the reason for disordered thresholds is ambiguous and is not clearly tied to category frequencies or average participant locations. Additional consideration of item content, rating scale category labels or descriptions, or other qualitative analyses may be needed to identify potential causes for the disordering and solutions to ensure that participants' interpretation of the scale categories reflects the intended order.

Table 3.2 shows the threshold location estimates from the RSM with their standard errors (SE) for the CES-D rating scale. The threshold estimates were ordered as expected on the logit scale such that

$\tau_1 = -0.30 < \tau_2 = -0.26 < \tau_3 = 0.55$. This result suggests that higher levels of depression were required for participants to respond in higher categories. These ordered thresholds also indicate a unimodal distribution of ratings across categories with a peak in the lowest category, as indicated by the percentage of ratings in each category. The empirical order of the threshold estimates matches the intended ordering. These results support the interpretation of lower ratings as indicators of less-severe depression and higher ratings as indicators of more-severe depression.

Ordering of Category Probability Curves

Graphical displays of rating scale category probabilities are a useful graphical tool for examining rating scale category ordering. Specifically, analysts can create plots of the conditional probability that a person with a given location estimate (θ) will provide a rating in each category of the scale. Figure 3.1 is an example of this type of graphical display based on the CES-D scale results. The *x*-axis shows person estimates from the RSM, and the *y*-axis represents a probability between 0 and 1. At each

Figure 3.1 Category Probability Curves Based on the Rating Scale Model

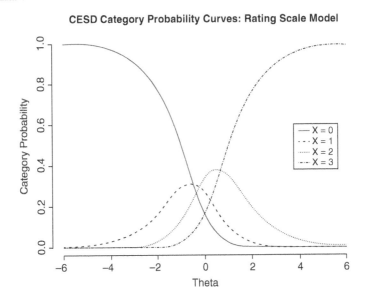

level on the x-axis, the four rating scale categories from the CES-D have a probability value, indicated by the height of their curve. If the rating scale categories are functioning in the intended order, participants with low levels of depression should be *likely* to respond in lower categories and *unlikely* to respond in higher categories. Likewise, participants with high levels of depression should be *likely* to respond in higher categories and *unlikely* to respond in lower categories.

The results in Figure 3.1 for the CES-D scale support the hypothesis that the rating scale categories are ordered as intended: As participant locations increase, the probability for a rating in higher categories also increases. This result provides further support for the conclusion that the CES-D rating scale categories are ordered as expected. The somewhat nondistinct curve for the second category ($x = 1$) will be examined in more detail with the next set of indices.

Rating Scale Category Precision

The second group of indicators helps researchers evaluate the distinctiveness of individual rating scale categories. *Rating scale category precision* indices allow researchers to determine whether each category can identify participants who have meaningfully different locations on the construct. In the context of the CES-D scale, category precision means that participants who respond in lower categories have notably lower levels of depression than participants who respond in higher categories.

Rating scale category precision indices are important because they help researchers evaluate how well each category works to identify participants who have different levels of the latent variable. For example, in the CES-D scale, rating scale precision indices tell researchers whether each of the four scale categories can identify people who have different levels of depression. As a result, these indicators provide actionable evidence to help analysts make decisions about the number of categories in their scale. For example, precision indices may indicate that the current scale categories are not very precise, and more categories are needed to distinguish among participants. Alternatively, precision indices may indicate that some categories reflect too-narrow a range of the construct to be useful. In these cases, fewer categories may be more appropriate. This information provides practical guidance for the development, revision, and interpretation of rating scales.

As with category ordering indicators, rating scale precision indicators are also important for evaluating rating scales that include neutral response options. For these instruments, researchers can use category precision analyses to determine whether the neutral category represents a meaningful level of the latent variable. If the neutral category is precise, this provides evidence that the scale is functioning as intended. If the neutral category is imprecise, analysts may decide to modify their scale by removing the neutral category or revising the description of categories to facilitate more meaningful responses. In other cases where it is not possible to collect new data, analysts may decide to recode responses such that the neutral category is combined with an adjacent category. Alternatively, some researchers opt to treat responses in the neutral category as missing data when precision indices suggest that it is not functioning well. This approach is possible with Rasch models because they function well in with missing data. Context-specific considerations should guide these decisions, and researchers should generally test several options before making these adjustments. We discuss these decisions further in Chapter 6.

Rasch models provide three major indices of rating scale category precision: distance between threshold locations on the logit scale, distinct category probability curves, and model-data fit within categories. We will consider each of these using results from the RSM analysis of the CES-D scale as an example.

Distance Between Threshold Location Estimates on the Logit Scale

One way to evaluate rating scale category precision is to examine the range of the latent variable that each category represents. With measurement models such as the RSM, this involves examining the distance on the logit scale between adjacent threshold location estimates (τ_k). For example, in the CES-D scale, which has three thresholds, we will examine the distance between the first two thresholds ($|\tau_2 - \tau_1|$) and the second and third threshold ($|\tau_3 - \tau_2|$). Very small differences may indicate that the rating scale categories do not provide distinct information about participants' levels of depression, whereas very large differences may indicate that the rating scale categories are not distinct enough to identify meaningful differences in depression. This information is important because it can help researchers evaluate the appropriateness of the length of their rating scale and adjust it as needed.

Table 3.2 gives the distance between rating scale category threshold locations based on the RSM analysis of the CES-D data. The absolute value of the distance between the first two thresholds ($|\tau_2 - \tau_1|$ = 0.04 logits)

56

as well as between the second and third threshold ($|\tau_3 - \tau_2| = 0.81$ logits) are relatively small. This result suggests that the middle categories in the CES-D rating scale may not discern meaningful differences among participants. Practically speaking, this finding suggests that fewer categories may be sufficient for the CES-D rating scale. Alternatively, the scale category labels may warrant revision in to more accurately identify participants with distinct levels of depression.

Practically speaking, analysts who calculate the distance between thresholds need guidance on determining whether the distances are too small, appropriate, or too large. Linacre (2002) described an approach for identifying the minimum distance on the logit scale between thresholds in cases where it is useful to interpret rating scale categories as a series of progressive steps.[1] Figure 3.2 shows these recommended values for scales with three to eleven categories. In addition, Linacre recommended that the maximum distance between rating scale category thresholds should always be less than 5 logits.

In the CES-D results in Table 3.2, the distance between the pairs of adjacent threshold values were both lower than Linacre's recommended distance for a four-category scale of approximately 1.10 logits. In practice, the necessary minimum and maximum distance between adjacent rating scale category thresholds will vary according to each

---

[1]This recommendation is based on situations where it may be desirable to interpret the rating scale as a set of dichotomous items, such as a developmental scale. In this case, the dichotomous items function as a set of Bernoulli (binomial) trials that are accomplished sequentially as participant locations on the latent variable increase. One can calculate adjacent categories (Rasch-Andrich) thresholds for the categories using the following equation:

$$\ln\left(\frac{x}{(m-x)+1}\right), \tag{3.1}$$

where ln is the natural logarithm, x is a category number, and the number of dichotomies is m. The number of dichotomies (m) is the number of categories in a rating scale minus 1. After finding the threshold value for each pair of adjacent categories, one can calculate the distance between them as a guideline for the minimum distance between thresholds. For example, in a scale with three categories ($x = 0, 1, 2$), the two thresholds are $\tau_1 = \ln(1/((2-1)+1)) = -0.693$ and $\tau_2 = \ln(2/((2-2)+1)) = -0.693$. With these values, the recommended minimum distance between categories is $\tau_2 - \tau_1 = 1.39$ logits.

Figure 3.2 Recommended Minimum Distance Between Adjacent Rating Scale Category Thresholds

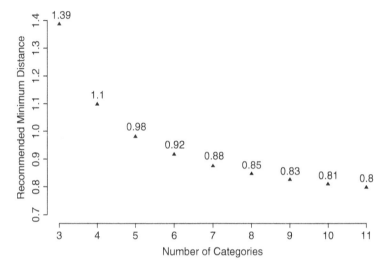

unique assessment context. In some applications where many distinctions are needed among participants, it may be important for each rating scale category to describe a relatively small range of logit-scale locations. For example, some latent variables may lend themselves to fine-grained distinctions between participants. In cases where targeted follow-up analyses or interventions are needed, researchers may wish to use more rating scale categories to make such distinctions. For example, if a survey was designed to identify participants with only the most-severe levels of depression, it may be useful to include enough categories to identify those participants.

In other applications where fewer distinctions are needed, it may be acceptable to include a wider range of locations within each category. For example, some latent variables may not lend themselves to fine-grained distinctions between participants, but rather reflect broader groups (e.g., low, moderate, and high levels of empathy). In other cases, surveys may serve as a starting place with which to make broad distinctions between participants prior to additional analyses. When this is the case, fewer categories may be sufficient.

Distinct Category Probability Curves

A second tool for evaluating category precision is to construct graphical displays of rating scale category probability curves (e.g., Figure 3.2) to evaluate whether each category in a rating scale has a unique range on the logit scale for which it is the most probable response. Category probability curves are useful in this context because they provide a visual display that researchers can use to understand and communicate the distinctiveness of the categories in their rating scale. If a rating scale category is not distinct, a visual display of category probability curves may reveal that it is *nonmodal*—in other words, the probability for the category is never higher than that of any other category. When this happens, the nonmodal category is not contributing to distinctions among participants with respect to the latent variable.

Returning to Figure 3.2, we see that the curve for the second rating scale category ($x = 1$) does not have a distinct range on the logit scale at which it is more probable than the other categories. This result suggests that there was no level of depression at which participants were most likely to respond in the second category—providing further evidence for imprecision of the middle categories for this instrument. In future administrations, analysts might consider using fewer rating scale categories or revising the scale category labels. Qualitative investigations such as cognitive interviews (Padilla & Leighton, 2017) may provide additional insight into potential explanations for the nondistinct category, as well as potentially useful revisions to the rating scale. In addition to discussing their interpretation of item stems, researchers who are interested in rating scale functioning could ask participants to report how they interpreted rating scale category labels or descriptions, and how they decided among rating scale categories when responding to each item.

Model-Data Fit for Rating Scale Categories

A third technique that researchers can use to evaluate rating scale category precision is to evaluate model-data fit (see Chapter 2) as it relates to rating scale categories. Although researchers who use Rasch models frequently evaluate model-data fit as it applies to items (e.g., Wu & Adams, 2013), persons (e.g., Smith, 1986; Walker & Engelhard, 2016), and explanatory facets such as raters (e.g., Wesolowski et al., 2015), researchers seldom conduct fit analyses specific to rating scale categories. Nonetheless, the same general techniques that are typically used to evaluate item, person, and facet fit can also be applied to evaluate model-data fit for rating scale categories.

Evidence of adequate model-data fit for rating scale categories suggests that the category is contributing to meaningful estimates of participant, item, and other facet locations on the construct. In contrast, substantial *misfit* means that the ratings observed within that category did not correspond to model expectations. Accordingly, the rating scale category is not contributing to interpretable measures of person, item, and other facet locations on the construct.

It is possible and sometimes useful to evaluate model-data fit using numeric fit statistics, such as Rasch model mean square error (MSE) fit statistics (Smith, 2004). However, the default settings in most popular standalone Rasch software programs (e.g., in Winsteps and Facets) only calculate the outfit formulation of MSE fit statistics for categories, or they do not report MSE fit statistics specific to rating scale categories. The same is also true for R packages that include Rasch model functions, such as the Extended Rasch Models (eRm) package (Mair et al., 2020) and the Test Analysis Modules (TAM) package (Robitzsch et al., 2020). Accordingly, we will focus on graphical displays for evaluating model-data fit related to rating scale categories.

Figure 3.3 is a plot of the empirical and expected item response function for the CES-D items based on the RSM. The x-axis shows participant locations relative to items, and the y-axis shows the CES-D rating scale categories. The dashed line with circles shows observed ratings, and the solid line shows RSM-expected ratings. Thin solid lines show a 95% confidence interval around the model-expected ratings. For ease of interpretation, light-dashed horizontal lines have been added to mark each of the CES-D rating scale categories ($x = 0, 1, 2, 3$).

The plot indicates that the ratings for the lower rating scale categories appear to correspond quite well to model expectations, because the empirical ratings were close to the expected ratings. However, there were some unexpected responses in the higher categories. These unexpected responses occurred when participants with relatively high depression levels gave lower-than-expected ratings. Although these deviations occurred, the empirical ratings were still quite close to the expected ratings. This finding provides support for the interpretation and use of the RSM estimates to analyze participant responses to the CES-D scale items. However, additional investigation of responses from participants who had relatively high levels of depression may provide useful insight to improve the utility of the CES-D scale among individuals with high levels of depression.

Figure 3.3 Expected and Empirical Item Response Function Based on the Rating Scale Model

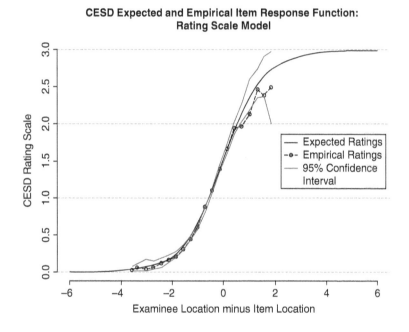

Rating Scale Category Comparability

The final set of rating scale analysis indices based on Rasch models provide information about the similarity of rating scale category functioning across elements of an assessment procedure. For example, it is often valuable to consider the degree to which a rating scale has a similar interpretation across individual items, subgroups of participants, or subsets of items. In the context of the CES-D scale, rating scale category comparability could be examined across participant subgroups. This analysis would provide insight into the comparability of ratings in each category between participants who have different demographic characteristics. Evidence of rating scale comparability between subgroups provides support for interpreting responses in a similar way for all participants.

The PCM and PC-MFRM make the comparison of rating scale functioning across elements of an assessment procedure relatively straightforward. However, the RSM does not facilitate these analyses.

Accordingly, we will revisit rating scale category comparability with the PCM and the PC-MFRM.

Rating Scale Analysis With the Partial Credit Model

In Chapter 2, we used the PCM to explore the psychometric properties of the CES-D data within a Rasch measurement framework, with an emphasis on fundamental measurement properties. Like the RSM, the PCM can also provide specific information related to rating scale functioning. Because the PCM includes separate threshold parameters (τ) for each item, this model allows researchers to consider details about rating scale functioning *specific to each item* (see Table 1.2). As a result, researchers who are interested in a detailed view of rating scale functioning specific to individual items may select the PCM. For the same reason, the PCM can also provide information about rating scale functioning in cases where the response scale is not consistent across all items. For example, if researchers need to analyze survey data that include different scale lengths across items, the PCM may be a useful choice.

In this section, we will use the CES-D data to consider how the PCM can provide information about rating scale functioning separately for individual items. Table 3.3 provides a summary of numeric results from the PCM rating scale analysis for selected items; Table A.3.1 in the Appendix for this chapter includes results for all items. Likewise, when indices involve graphical displays, results are shown for selected items for the sake of brevity. In practice, one would examine all of the indices for all of the items in an analysis.

Category Ordering Indices

Average Participant Locations Within Rating Scale Categories for Individual Items

We will start to examine the CES-D scale data for evidence of category ordering by calculating the average location for participants (θ) who responded in each of the rating scale categories. In contrast to the RSM analyses, we will calculate this value specific to each item in the PCM analysis.

Table 3.3 shows the average location estimate from the PCM for participants who responded in each category of the CES-D rating scale, specific to individual items. The average participant location estimates

Table 3.3 Rating Scale Category Calibrations From the PCM (Selected Items)

| Item | Rating Scale Category | % of Ratings | Average Participant Location Estimate (θ) | Threshold Location | | Absolute Distance Between Adjacent Threshold Estimates |
				Threshold Estimate (τ)	Standard Error	
1	0	30%	−1.12	N/A	N/A	N/A
	1	40%	−0.89	−1.30	0.08	N/A
	2	26%	−0.54	−0.25	0.08	1.05
	3	4%	−0.02	1.55	0.18	1.80
2	0	50%	−1.11	N/A	N/A	N/A
	1	25%	−0.74	−0.20	0.08	N/A
	2	17%	−0.34	−0.20	0.09	0.00
	3	8%	−0.17	0.40	0.13	0.60
3	0	60%	−1.09	N/A	N/A	N/A
	1	17%	−0.70	0.34	0.08	N/A
	2	13%	−0.49	−0.28[a]	0.09	0.62
	3	10%	−0.04	−0.07	0.13	0.21
12	0	32%	−0.74	N/A	N/A	N/A
	1	29%	−0.49	−0.55	0.08	N/A
	2	28%	−0.29	−0.33	0.08	0.22
	3	11%	−0.08	0.88	0.12	1.21
13	0	44%	−1.25	N/A	N/A	N/A
	1	27%	−0.98	−0.59	0.08	N/A
	2	24%	−0.54	−0.64[a]	0.08	0.05
	3	5%	−0.29	1.23	0.17	1.87
15	0	45%	−1.11	N/A	N/A	N/A
	1	29%	−0.84	−0.54	0.08	N/A
	2	19%	−0.49	−0.20	0.09	0.34
	3	6%	−0.21	0.74	0.15	0.94
20	0	45%	−1.13	N/A	N/A	N/A
	1	32%	−0.75	−0.60	0.08	N/A
	2	16%	−0.44	0.12	0.09	0.72
	3	7%	−0.07	0.48	0.14	0.36

[a]Disordered threshold.
Note: The Appendix includes results for all CES-D scale items.

(θ) increased as the categories progressed from low ($x = 0$) to high ($x = 3$) for all items. Congruent with the overall results from the RSM, these results suggest that participants' level of depression corresponded to their use of the CES-D rating scale categories. That is, participants who had less-severe depression used lower rating scale categories more often, and participants with more-severe depression used higher rating scale categories more often. The PCM results indicate that this pattern was true for each item in the CES-D scale.

Logit-Scale Location Estimates of Rating Scale Category Thresholds for Individual Items

Next, we will examine item-specific rating scale category thresholds for evidence that the observed order corresponds with our expected order. Table 3.3 shows item-specific rating scale category threshold location estimates from the PCM with their standard errors. For most of the items, the threshold estimates were ordered as expected such that $\tau_1 < \tau_2 < \tau_3$. This result indicates generally appropriate category ordering: Lower categories in the CES-D rating scale corresponded to lower levels of depression, and higher categories correspond to higher levels of depression.

However, the threshold locations also revealed some differences related to category ordering specific to individual items. For example, for Item 2, the first and second thresholds had equivalent locations ($\tau_1 = \tau_2 = 0.20$). This result suggests that although the categories were not disordered, they did not reflect different levels of depression. We explore this result further in our rating scale category precision analyses with the PCM.

In addition, ten items (Items 3, 4, 8, 9, 10, 11, 13, 14, 17, and 20) had *dis*ordering between two thresholds. For these items, there was a mismatch between the intended order and participants' actual interpretation of the CES-D rating scale categories. Practically, this result suggests that for some items, higher rating scale categories did not always indicate increasing levels of depression for these items. We did not detect this item-specific category disordering with the RSM.

Ordering of Category Probability Curves for Individual Items

Next, we will use graphical displays of rating scale category probabilities as additional evidence of rating scale category ordering. Figure 3.4 is a plot of item-specific rating scale category probability curves for selected items that show different patterns of rating scale category ordering. For example, the plots for Item 1 and Item 15 show category probability curves that are ordered as expected. The

Figure 3.4 Category Probability Curves Based on the Partial Credit Model

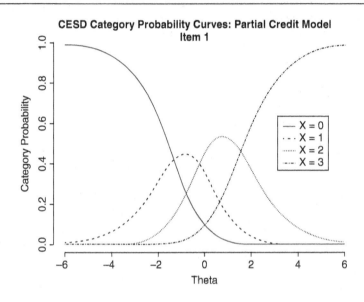

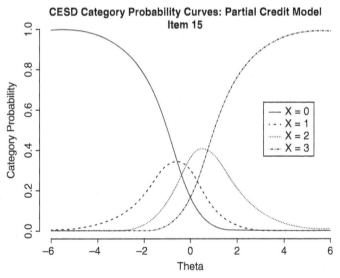

(Continued)

Figure 3.4 Category Probability Curves Based on the Partial Credit Model *(Continued)*

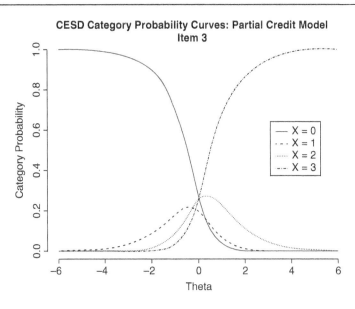

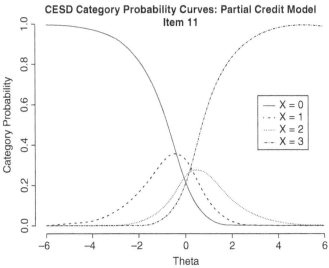

probabilities for each scale category increase and decrease successively as the logit scale moves from low to high. In the context of the CES-D scale, this means that the lower rating scale categories correspond to lower levels of depression and higher rating scale categories correspond to higher levels of depression. These plots are evidence of appropriate category ordering specific to individual items (in this case, Items 1 and 15).

In contrast, the plot for Item 3 shows *dis*ordered rating scale category thresholds for the second and third thresholds. For Item 3, the point at which the line for the first category ($x = 0$) intersects with the line for the second category ($x = 1$; i.e., τ_1) is located *higher* on the logit scale than the point at which the line for the second category ($x = 1$) intersects with the line for the third category ($x = 2$; τ_2). The plot for Item 11 shows a similar result, where $\tau_2 > \tau_3$. These results highlight differences in category ordering across individual items in the CES-D scale. We will examine and discuss these results in more detail with the category precision indicators from the PCM.

It is interesting to note that conclusions about category ordering based on thresholds and graphical displays of category probabilities were different from the conclusions based on average participant locations within categories. These indices provide different perspectives on category ordering that are not always perfectly aligned. Evidence of category disordering based on *any* indicator suggests that additional investigation and consideration is warranted to understand rating scale functioning.

Rating Scale Category Precision

Distance Between Rating Scale Category Threshold Location Estimates on the Logit Scale for Individual Items

Table 3.3 shows the distance between rating scale category threshold locations based on the PCM. The absolute value of the distance between the first two thresholds ($|\tau_2 - \tau_1|$) are smaller than Linacre's (2002) recommended minimum value of approximately 1.1 logits (see Chapter 2) for all items except Item 17. In addition, the absolute distance between the second and third thresholds ($|\tau_3 - \tau_2|$) falls below 1.1 logits for all items except Items 1, 5, 12, 13, and 15. These relatively small distances between thresholds for most of the items suggest that the middle rating scale categories scale may not discern meaningful differences among participants. As a result, researchers may consider revising the scale length or rating scale category labels in future administrations of the CES-D scale.

Distinct Rating Scale Category Probability Curves
for Individual Items

Returning to Figure 3.4, we will now consider the rating scale category probability curves from the perspective of category precision. The curves for Item 1 indicate that all four rating scale categories have a distinct range on the latent variable at which they are the most probable. In other words, each category reflects a unique level of depression for most of the CES-D scale items. Although the distance between the adjacent thresholds was less than 1.1 logits, the graphical display indicates that the rating scale categories reflect distinct ranges on the logit scale. On the other hand, the category probability curves for Item 3 and Item 11 clearly indicate that the middle categories ($x = 1$ and $x = 2$) do not have a distinct range on the logit scale at which they are more probable than the other categories. This result provides further evidence that the middle categories for the CES-D rating scale may not always provide unique information about participants' depression levels. The interpretation of the category probability curves for Item 15 is less straightforward. Although there is a distinct range on the logit scale at which $x = 1$ is most probable, this range is very small, and it suggests a potential threat to category precision for this item.

Graphical Model-Data Fit Displays for Categories
for Individual Items

Finally, we will evaluate rating scale category precision using graphical displays of residuals and model-expected responses for individual items. Figure 3.5 is a plot of the empirical and expected item response function for four selected CES-D items based on the PCM. These plots use the same format as those in Figure 3.3, but they are unique to the item listed in the title for each plot.

For each of the items in this figure, the empirical and expected item response functions suggest generally acceptable model-data fit, because the pattern of observed ratings deviates only slightly from the expected ratings and the unexpected ratings do not exceed the 95% confidence interval for model expectations. However, it is interesting to note that the locations and magnitude of unexpected responses varied across items.

Figure 3.5 Expected and Empirical Item Response Functions Based on the Partial Credit Model

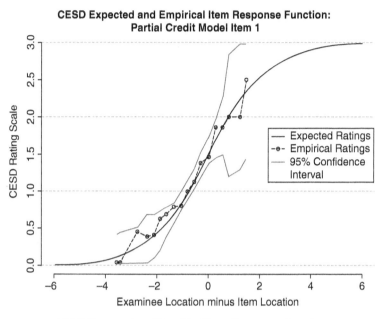

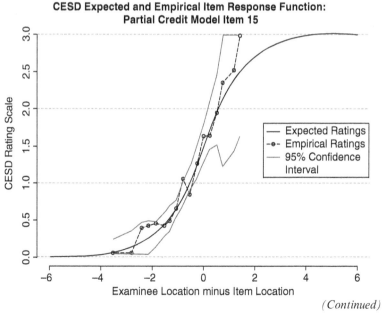

(Continued)

Figure 3.5 Expected and Empirical Item Response Functions Based on the Partial Credit Model *(Continued)*

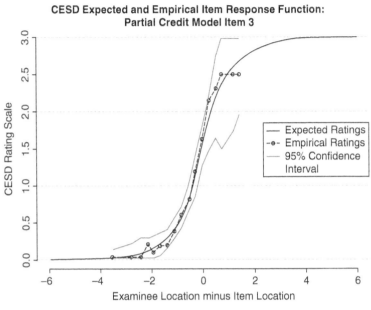

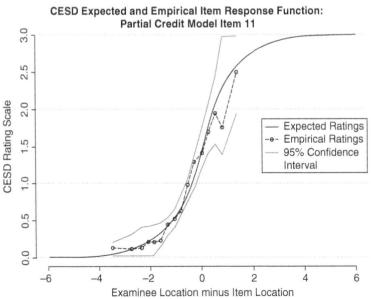

Rating Scale Category Comparability

The PCM provides information about rating scale functioning specific to each item in the scale. As a result, researchers can compare the results from category ordering and category precision indices to evaluate whether rating scale functioning is comparable across items. This information can help researchers determine whether it is appropriate to interpret responses in a similar way across items. For example, in the CES-D scale, comparisons between items can help researchers ensure that responses in category 2 (*Some or a little of the time*) can be interpreted in the same way between items. In addition, PCM analyses help researchers evaluate whether the difference between categories, such as comparisons of responses in category 2 to category 3 (*Occasionally or a moderate amount of time*), reflect the same difference in the severity of depression levels between items.

In our PCM analysis of the CES-D scale, we examined category ordering indices separately for each item. From the threshold location estimates and graphical displays of rating scale category probabilities, we saw that there were some differences in category ordering between items. Specifically, the PCM identified disordered rating scale category thresholds for some, but not all items in the scale (see Table 3.3). This result suggests that participants may have interpreted the order of the rating scale categories differently for individual items. For example, the PCM results suggested that the categories were ordered as expected for Item 1, but not for Item 3.

We also examined category precision indices separately for each item in the CES-D scale. From the perspective of category comparability, researchers can use these results to examine whether the structure of the rating scale is similar across individual items. For example, we used results from the PCM to calculate the absolute value of the distance between rating scale category thresholds for each item (see Table 3.3). We can compare these values across items to evaluate whether the relative distance on the latent variable (e.g., the difference in depression levels) between categories is similar across items. The results in Table 3.3 clearly indicate that the distance between rating scale category thresholds was different between items in the CES-D scale. For example, the distance between the second and third threshold was more than twice as large for Item 1 (1.80) as it was for Item 2 (0.60). This result suggests that there was a larger difference in the level of depression between participants who responded in category 2 (*Some or a little of the* time) and category 3 (*Most or all of the time*) for Item 1 than for Item 2.

Together, the category comparability analyses with the **PCM** suggest that the CES-D rating scale functions differently across items. These results support the use of a measurement model that directly models differences in the structure of the rating scale for individual items, such as the PCM. Whereas the RSM provided an overall summary of rating scale functioning, the PCM identified item-level differences in rating scale functioning. Researchers can use this approach to identify and describe the nature of the differences in rating scale functioning between items, and to identify specific items that warrant further consideration and revision.

Rating Scale Analyses With the Partial Credit Many-Facet Rasch Model

In Chapter 2, we used the PC-MFRM to explore the psychometric properties of the CES-D data within a Rasch measurement framework, with an emphasis on fundamental measurement properties. We saw that the PC-MFRM can extend the PCM by providing details about explanatory variables (i.e., facets) that are unique to specific assessment contexts.

The PC-MFRM can also provide specific information related to rating scale functioning. Because the PC-MFRM includes explanatory facets, we can use it to consider differences in rating scale functioning related to levels of those facets, such as subgroups of participants or subsets of items (see Table 1.2 and Table 3.1). Accordingly, the PC-MFRM allows us to examine the comparability of rating scale functioning between subsets of participants and subsets of items.

Comparability of rating scale functioning between participant subgroups is a different type of analysis than overall comparisons of the level of a construct between subgroups. In previous studies, some researchers (e.g., Perreira et al., 2005) have examined subgroup-related differences in the internal structure of the CES-D. However, these analyses have not considered subgroup differences specific to rating scale category ordering and precision. The PC-MFRM facilitates this type of analysis.

For continuity with Chapter 2, we use the PC-MFRM in which rating scale thresholds are estimated separately for each education level subgroup (Equation 2.16). This model allows us to examine rating scale functioning in detail for participants with different levels of educational attainment. Specifically, we compare rating scale functioning across the education-level subgroups.

Category Ordering Indices

Average Participant Locations Within Rating Scale Categories for Levels of Explanatory Facet(s)

Continuing our exploration of rating scale category ordering, we will examine the average estimated location for participants who responded in each rating scale category. When we use the PC-MFRM, we can examine these values within levels of the explanatory facet of interest. In our example, we examine average participant locations within rating scale categories separately for the education-level subgroups.

Table 3.4 shows the average location estimates from the PC-MFRM for participants who responded in each category of the CES-D rating scale, specific to each education-level subgroup. The average estimates increase monotonically (i.e., they do not decrease) as the categories

Table 3.4   Rating Scale Category Calibrations From the PC-MFRM

| Education Level | Rating Scale Category | % of Ratings | Average Participant Location Estimate (θ) | Threshold Location | | Absolute Distance Between Adjacent Threshold Estimates |
				Threshold Estimate (τ)	Standard Error	
Eighth Grade or Less	0	83%	−2.12	N/A	N/A	N/A
	1	13%	−1.87	−0.11	0.19	N/A
	2	4%	−1.18	−0.37	0.37	0.18
	3	1%	−1.37	0.49	1.01	0.64
Some High School	0	45%	−1.08	N/A	N/A	N/A
	1	23%	−0.63	−0.17	0.06	N/A
	2	22%	−0.29	−0.45	0.06	0.00
	3	10%	0.01	0.62	0.09	0.03
High School or Equivalent	0	47%	−1.09	N/A	N/A	N/A
	1	27%	−0.71	−0.32	0.03	N/A
	2	18%	−0.41	−0.21	0.03	0.00
	3	8%	−0.20	0.54	0.05	0.02
Some College or	0	48%	−1.07	N/A	N/A	N/A
	1	26%	−0.74	−0.28	0.03	N/A

(Continued)

Table 3.4 Rating Scale Category Calibrations From the
PC-MFRM *(Continued)*

Education Level	Rating Scale Category	% of Ratings	Average Participant Location Estimate (θ)	Threshold Estimate (τ)	Standard Error	Absolute Distance Between Adjacent Threshold Estimates
				Threshold Location		
Two-Year Degree	2	18%	−0.41	−0.25	0.03	0.00
	3	8%	−0.13	0.53	0.05	0.02
Four-Year Degree	0	47%	−1.05	N/A	N/A	N/A
	1	27%	−0.78	−0.36	0.05	N/A
	2	18%	−0.45	−0.24	0.06	0.01
	3	7%	−0.16	0.60	0.10	0.04
Graduate or Professional Degree	0	42%	−0.83	N/A	N/A	N/A
	1	29%	−0.64	−0.36	0.09	N/A
	2	21%	−0.40	−0.22	0.09	0.00
	3	9%	−0.22	0.59	0.15	0.06

progress from low ($x = 0$) to high ($x = 3$) for almost all of the subgroups. An exception occurs for participants in the *8th Grade or Less* education level subgroup. For this subgroup, participants who responded in category 3 (*Occasionally or a moderate amount of time*) had lower locations on the logit scale (i.e., less depression), on average, than participants who responded in category 2 (*Some or a little of the time*). This result provides additional evidence that the rating scale category ordering is not consistent across participants with different levels of education. Additional research may be needed to understand these differences.

Logit-Scale Location Estimates of Rating Scale Category Thresholds for Elements of Explanatory Facet(s)

Next, we will examine rating scale threshold locations specific to each element of the explanatory facet of interest. In our analysis, the explanatory facet is education subgroups, so we will evaluate the degree to which the rating scale category thresholds are ordered as expected for the six education-level subgroups in our example data.

Table 3.4 shows subgroup-specific threshold location estimates from the PC-MFRM with their standard errors for the CES-D data. For all of the subgroups except *8th Grade or Less* and *Some High School*, the rating scale category threshold estimates were ordered as expected such that $\tau_1 < \tau_2 < \tau_3$. However, for participants in the *8th Grade or Less* and *Some High School* subgroups, the PC-MFRM detected threshold disordering between τ_1 and τ_2. For these participants, there was a mismatch between the intended order of the categories and participants' actual interpretation and use of the categories. This result suggests that category ordering was not consistent for participants with different levels of education. Additional research may be warranted to better understand these differences.

Ordering of Category Probability Curves for Levels of Explanatory Facet(s)

With the PC-MFRM, we can examine plots of rating scale category probabilities within levels of an explanatory facet for evidence of rating scale category ordering. In our analysis, we will examine these plots specific to education-level subgroups.

Figure 3.6 is a plot of category probability curves for the six education-level subgroups. For the *8th Grade or Less* and *Some High School* subgroups, the category probability curves show disordering between the second and third rating scale categories ($\tau_1 > \tau_2$). Although there are some differences in their patterns, the category probability curves are ordered as expected for the other subgroups. Together with the other category ordering indices, these results further confirm the finding that the order of the CES-D rating scale categories is not consistent among education-level subgroups, and that participants with lower education levels interpret the order of the rating scale categories differently from the other subgroups. We will examine these plots in more detail as part of the category precision analyses.

Rating Scale Category Precision

Distance Between Threshold Location Estimates on the Logit Scale for Levels of Explanatory Facet(s)

Next, we will examine the distance between adjacent rating scale category thresholds as an indicator of rating scale category precision. Because we are using the PC-MFRM, we can examine this indicator separately for levels of our explanatory facet: Education-level subgroups.

Figure 3.6 Category Probability Curves Based on the PC-MFRM

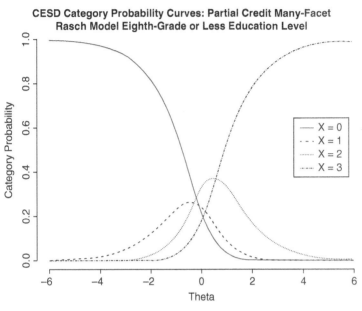

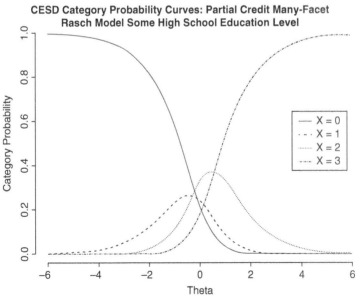

(Continued)

Figure 3.6 Category Probability Curves Based on the PC-MFRM
(Continued)

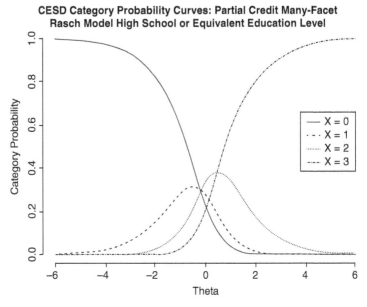

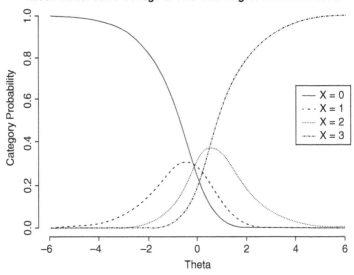

(Continued)

Figure 3.6 Category Probability Curves Based on the PC-MFRM
(Continued)

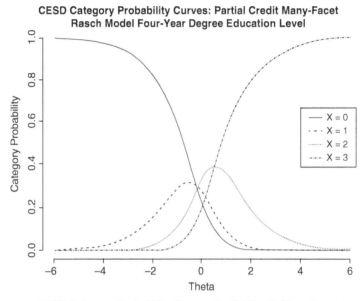

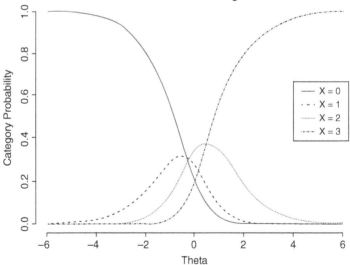

78

Table 3.4 presents the distance between rating scale category threshold locations based on the PC-MFRM analysis of the CES-D data. The absolute value of the distance between the first two thresholds ($|\tau_2 - \tau_1|$) as well as between the second and third thresholds ($|\tau_3 - \tau_2|$) are relatively small and fall below Linacre's (2002) recommended minimum of 1.1 logits (see Figure 3.2). These relatively small distances between thresholds suggest that, when considered separately by subgroup, the middle rating scale categories in the CES-D rating scale may not discern meaningful differences among participants. Although the distances between thresholds varied across the participant subgroups, the general conclusion of relatively indistinct middle rating scale categories was common for all subgroups. This result suggests that additional consideration of the scale length and rating scale category descriptions may be warranted to ensure that the CES-D rating scale can identify participants with distinct levels of depression.

Distinct Category Probability Curves

Returning to Figure 3.6, we will now consider the rating scale category probability curves from the perspective of category precision. These plots indicate that, when examined by subgroup, the middle rating scale categories ($x = 1$ and $x = 2$) do not have a distinct range on the logit scale at which they are more probable than the other categories. This result provides additional evidence for imprecision of the middle categories for the CES-D rating scale within education-level subgroups.

Graphical Model-Data Fit Displays for Categories
for Levels of Explanatory Facet(s)

Finally, we will use graphical displays to evaluate rating scale category precision from the perspective of model-data fit. With the PC-MFRM, we can construct and evaluate these displays separately for levels of our explanatory facet(s). In our example, we will examine graphical model-data fit displays for each education-level subgroup.

Figure 3.7 is a plot of the empirical and expected item response functions for the six education-level subgroups; these plots are unique for each education-level subgroup. The plot for each subgroup shows a different pattern of expected and unexpected ratings. Although there are instances of model-data misfit for all of the subgroups, the location on the logit scale and the direction of the unexpected ratings are different. For example, there were unexpectedly high ratings among

Figure 3.7 Expected and Empirical Response Functions Based on the PC-MFRM

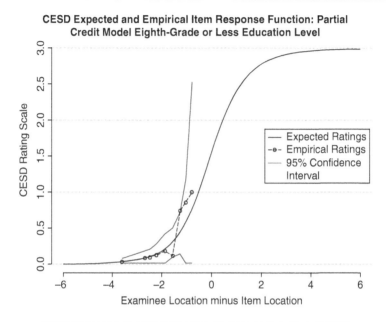

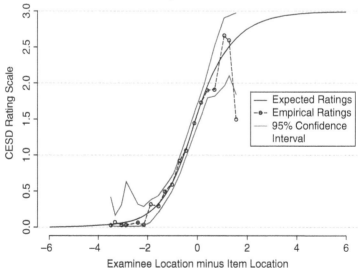

Figure 3.7 Expected and Empirical Response Functions Based on the PC-MFRM *(Continued)*

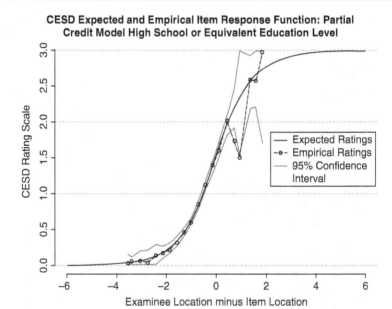

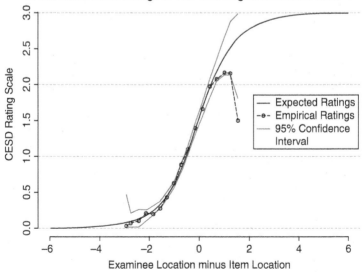

(Continued)

Figure 3.7 Expected and Empirical Response Functions Based on the PC-MFRM *(Continued)*

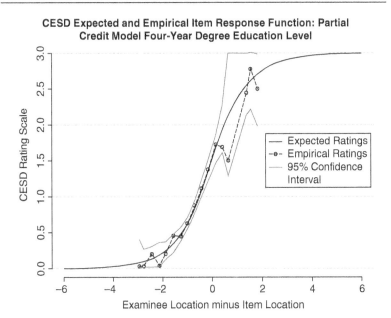

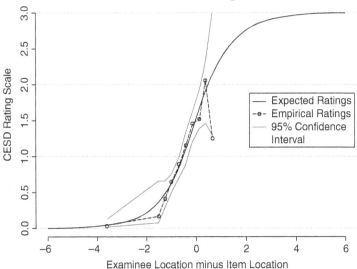

participants with relatively high levels of depression who were in the *High School or Equivalent* and in the *Four-Year Degree* subgroups. On the other hand, there were unexpectedly low ratings among participants with relatively high levels of depression who were in the *Some High School* and *Some College or Two-Year Degree* subgroups. Despite some differences across subgroups, these results indicate generally close alignment between model expectations and the observed ratings—thus providing support for the interpretation of the PC-MFRM estimates.

Chapter Summary

This chapter began with an overview of rating scale analysis indices based on polytomous Rasch measurement theory models. Three major sets of indices were presented that researchers can use to evaluate rating scale functioning with polytomous Rasch models: (1) indices of category ordering, (2) indices of category precision, and (3) indices of rating scale comparability. The example CES-D dataset was used to illustrate in detail how to conduct and interpret results from rating scale analyses with the RSM, PCM, and PC-MFRM. Each model provided unique insight into rating scale functioning for the example CES-D data.

First, the RSM provided an overall view of rating scale functioning across all of the CES-D items and participants. Researchers may prefer the RSM for rating scale analysis when they need a relatively simple or overarching picture of rating scale functioning, and details about individual items are not necessary or practical. In addition, researchers may prefer the RSM if, after applying the PCM, they find that rating scale functioning is generally comparable across items. In this case, the RSM is a more parsimonious model that is simpler to interpret and explain.

Next, the PCM provided item-specific information about rating scale functioning for each item in the CES-D. Researchers may prefer the PCM when they want to examine rating scale functioning in detail specific to each item in their analysis. The PCM is also a useful option when the response scale varies across items, or when there is reason to believe that participants will use the scale differently for different items or sets of items. Finally, researchers may prefer the PCM when they apply it and find that rating scale functioning was notably different across items. In this case, the PCM allows them to capture these differences in rating scale ordering and precision in their analysis.

Finally, we used the PC-MFRM to explore rating scale functioning specific to participant subgroups. The PC-MFRM provides an in-depth examination of rating scale functioning that is customizable to reflect explanatory variables (facets) relevant to each assessment context. In our example, we considered differences in rating scale functioning related to participants' level of education. The PC-MFRM highlighted differences in rating scale category ordering and precision between participants who had different levels of education. In practice, researchers may prefer the PC-MFRM when they want to ensure that subgroups of participants interpret and use a rating scale in a comparable way. Evidence that rating scales function appropriately for all subgroups provides support for other comparisons between subgroups, such as total score comparisons or differential item functioning analyses, which may be an important part of validity analyses. In addition, researchers may select the PC-MFRM when they want to ensure that the internal structure of their instrument is comparable across sets of items or sections of a survey. In this case, one could specify the rating scale structure to vary across item subsets.

Each of the Rasch models illustrated in this chapter provides unique information that can help researchers evaluate rating scale functioning for their surveys and identify areas and directions for revision. In the next chapter, we consider non-Rasch models that can also provide insight into rating scale functioning.

APPENDIX

Table A.3.1 Rating Scale Category Calibrations From the PCM: All CES-D Scale Items

Item	Rating Scale Category	% of Ratings	Average Participant Location Estimate (θ)	Threshold Estimate (τ)	Standard Error	Absolute Distance Between Adjacent Threshold Estimates
1	0	30%	−1.12	N/A	N/A	N/A
	1	40%	−0.89	−1.30	0.08	N/A
	2	26%	−0.54	−0.25	0.08	1.05
	3	4%	−0.02	1.55	0.18	1.80
2	0	50%	−1.11	N/A	N/A	N/A
	1	25%	−0.74	−0.20	0.08	N/A
	2	17%	−0.34	−0.20	0.09	0.00
	3	8%	−0.17	0.40	0.13	0.60
3	0	60%	−1.09	N/A	N/A	N/A
	1	17%	−0.70	0.34	0.08	N/A
	2	13%	−0.49	−0.28[a]	0.09	0.62
	3	10%	−0.04	−0.07	0.13	0.21
4	0	51%	−1.00	N/A	N/A	N/A
	1	22%	−0.67	0.01	0.08	N/A
	2	18%	−0.38	−0.32[a]	0.09	0.33
	3	10%	−0.15	0.31	0.12	0.63
5	0	40%	−1.31	N/A	N/A	N/A
	1	32%	−0.91	−0.86	0.08	N/A
	2	24%	−0.54	−0.47	0.08	0.39
	3	4%	−0.03	1.33	0.18	1.80
6	0	51%	−1.15	N/A	N/A	N/A
	1	25%	−0.82	−0.26	0.08	N/A
	2	16%	−0.43	−0.21	0.09	0.05
	3	7%	−0.12	0.47	0.14	0.68

(Continued)

Table A.3.1 Rating Scale Category Calibrations From the PCM: All CES-D Scale Items *(Continued)*

Item	Rating Scale Category	% of Ratings	Average Participant Location Estimate (θ)	Threshold Estimate (τ)	Standard Error	Absolute Distance Between Adjacent Threshold Estimates
7	0	47%	−1.07	N/A	N/A	N/A
	1	27%	−0.71	−0.30	0.08	N/A
	2	17%	−0.41	−0.12	0.09	0.18
	3	9%	0.02	0.41	0.13	0.53
8	0	44%	−0.84	N/A	N/A	N/A
	1	21%	−0.52	0.05	0.08	N/A
	2	21%	−0.32	−0.40[a]	0.08	0.45
	3	13%	−0.01	0.36	0.11	0.76
9	0	56%	−1.08	N/A	N/A	N/A
	1	22%	−0.71	0.04	0.08	N/A
	2	13%	−0.48	−0.08[a]	0.09	0.12
	3	9%	−0.15	0.05	0.13	0.13
10	0	53%	−1.16	N/A	N/A	N/A
	1	22%	−0.82	−0.08	0.08	N/A
	2	19%	−0.44	−0.51[a]	0.09	0.43
	3	7%	−0.16	0.58	0.14	1.09
11	0	49%	−1.09	N/A	N/A	N/A
	1	30%	−0.72	−0.41	0.08	N/A
	2	13%	−0.29	0.29	0.09	0.70
	3	9%	−0.24	0.12[a]	0.13	0.17
12	0	32%	-0.74	N/A	N/A	N/A
	1	29%	−0.49	−0.55	0.08	N/A
	2	28%	−0.29	−0.33	0.08	0.22
	3	11%	−0.08	0.88	0.12	1.21
13	0	44%	−1.25	N/A	N/A	N/A
	1	27%	−0.98	−0.59	0.08	N/A
	2	24%	−0.54	−0.64[a]	0.08	0.05
	3	5%	−0.29	1.23	0.17	1.87

(Continued)

Table A.3.1 Rating Scale Category Calibrations From the PCM: All CES-D Scale Items *(Continued)*

Item	Rating Scale Category	% of Ratings	Average Participant Location Estimate (θ)	Threshold Estimate (τ)	Standard Error	Absolute Distance Between Adjacent Threshold Estimates
14	0	55%	−1.17	N/A	N/A	N/A
	1	20%	−0.76	0.05	0.08	N/A
	2	17%	−0.44	−0.49[a]	0.09	0.54
	3	8%	−0.14	0.44	0.14	0.93
15	0	45%	−1.11	N/A	N/A	N/A
	1	29%	−0.84	−0.54	0.08	N/A
	2	19%	−0.49	−0.20	0.09	0.34
	3	6%	−0.21	0.74	0.15	0.94
16	0	37%	−0.80	N/A	N/A	N/A
	1	27%	−0.63	−0.42	0.08	N/A
	2	25%	−0.30	−0.34	0.08	0.08
	3	10%	−0.15	0.76	0.12	1.10
17	0	64%	−1.03	N/A	N/A	N/A
	1	12%	−0.67	0.78	0.08	N/A
	2	12%	−0.43	−0.50[a]	0.09	1.28
	3	12%	−0.17	−0.28	0.12	0.22
18	0	42%	−1.24	N/A	N/A	N/A
	1	36%	−0.82	−0.87	0.08	N/A
	2	17%	−0.51	0.09	0.09	0.96
	3	5%	−0.14	0.78	0.16	0.69
19	0	53%	−1.10	N/A	N/A	N/A
	1	20%	−0.73	0.09	0.08	N/A
	2	18%	−0.44	−0.53[a]	0.09	0.62
	3	9%	−0.11	0.44	0.13	0.97
20	0	45%	−1.13	N/A	N/A	N/A
	1	32%	−0.75	−0.60	0.08	N/A
	2	16%	−0.44	0.12	0.09	0.72
	3	7%	−0.07	0.48	0.14	0.36

[a]Disordered threshold.

4 NON-RASCH IRT MODELS FOR RATING SCALE ANALYSIS

In addition to the Rasch models presented in Chapters 2 and 3, it is also possible to conduct rating scale analysis using non-Rasch IRT models. This chapter provides an overview and illustration of two major types of non-Rasch models that researchers can use to conduct rating scale analysis: (1) polytomous IRT models with slope parameters; and (2) polytomous IRT models with a cumulative probability formulation.

As shown in Table 1.2, researchers typically select non-Rasch models for rating scale analysis when their overall modeling goals include *describing* the characteristics of their data, such as differences in item slope (i.e., discrimination; discussed further in the next section), rather than *evaluating* the characteristics of their data against requirements based on a theoretical framework for measurement. Situations that may call for this non-Rasch approach include contexts where researchers do not wish to identify problematic characteristics to inform revisions to their measurement instrument, when researchers wish to obtain a detailed representation of the characteristics of their data for use in other statistical analyses, or when it is not necessary to establish a single item and person hierarchy to represent a construct. Other times, researchers may wish to apply non-Rasch models to their survey data to learn about its characteristics before selecting a final model.

Table 4.1 applies the first two groups of rating scale analysis indicators (rating scale category ordering and rating scale category precision) to the models that are discussed in this chapter. The general motivation and use of these indicators is similar between polytomous Rasch models and the non-Rasch models in this chapter, with some differences related to the characteristics of each model. However, rating scale category comparability cannot be directly evaluated using the models in this chapter besides comparisons between items. Because the formulation of each of the selected non-Rasch models is unique, rating scale analysis indicators are presented separately for each model using analyses of the CES-D scale data as an example. Annotated statistical software syntax for each model is provided in the online supplement at **https://study.sagepub.com/researchmethods/qass/wind-exploring-rating-scale-functioning**.

87

Table 4.1 Overview of Rating Scale Category Functioning Indices Based on Non-Rasch IRT Models

| | | Polytomous IRT With Slope Parameter | Polytomous IRT With Cumulative Probability Formulation |
| | | Generalized Partial Credit Model | Graded Response Model |
Groups of Indices	Guiding Question		
Rating scale category ordering	To what extent do higher rating scale categories indicate higher locations on the construct?	Ordering indices specific to individual items	Categories are ordered by definition
Rating scale category precision	To what extent do individual rating scale categories reflect distinct ranges on the construct?	Precision indices specific to individual items	Precision indices specific to individual items

Rating Scale Analysis Using Polytomous IRT Models With Slope Parameters

The first category of non-Rasch models for this chapter is polytomous IRT models that include slope (i.e., discrimination) parameters. These models directly incorporate differences in the *slope* of item response functions (see Figure 2.3), or the degree to which items distinguish among participants with different locations on the latent variable, into their estimation procedure. The major practical implication of modeling item slopes is that analysts can identify items that have notable differences in the degree to which they distinguish among participants with different locations on the latent variable. For example, items with very low discrimination are those on which participants tend to respond in the same way regardless of their location on the construct. Items with very high discrimination clearly separate participants into distinct groups related to their locations on the construct. Researchers often prefer items that have moderate levels of discrimination. In Rasch models (Chapter 3), items that have extreme high or low levels of discrimination would likely be flagged with residual-based fit statistics.

Researchers generally use polytomous IRT models with slope parameters because these models reflect differences in item discrimination that often occur in real-world applications of rating scale instruments. In practical survey research, some items distinguish (i.e., discriminate) between participants more effectively than others. For example, in the CES-D scale, it is plausible to assume that some items, such as Item 9: *I thought my life had been a failure*, may be more effective at distinguishing between depression levels than other items, such as Item 15: *People were unfriendly*. Figure 4.1 illustrates these differences in discrimination. The x-axis is the theta (θ) scale that represents depression, and the y-axis shows the CES-D rating scale. The solid line shows the expected item response function (IRF) for Item 9 and the dashed line shows the expected IRF for Item 15. These IRFs were constructed with item slope parameters included in the estimation. We can see differences in item slope between these two items, where the IRF for Item 9 is steeper compared to the IRF for Item 15.

Figure 4.1 Expected Item Response Functions That Include Item Slope Parameters

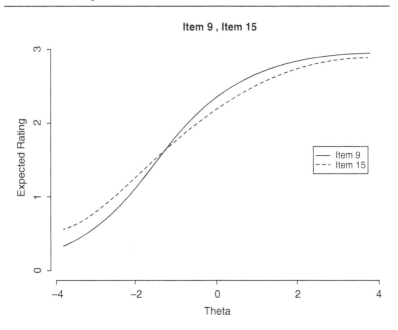

When differences in item discrimination are included in an IRT model, this means that the relative order of the items might not be the same for all participants (see Figure 4.1). Models that include slope parameters take these differences into account when estimating person and item locations. In a sense, deciding between non-Rasch models and IRT models that include slope parameters reflects a tradeoff between a simple, person-invariant item order that facilitates a clear representation of a construct (Rasch approach) where differences in item discrimination are flagged as misfit and model estimates that may more closely reflect patterns in the data (slope parameter approach), but that do not alert researchers to failures of invariance that may complicate interpretation.

Generalized Partial Credit Model

The Generalized Partial Credit Model (GPCM; Muraki, 1997) is a polytomous IRT model with a slope parameter. The GPCM can be used to model ordinal item response data with three or more categories, such as responses to Likert-type survey items. As shown in Table 1.2, researchers typically choose the GPCM when their analytic goals are not necessarily related to evaluating their data for adherence to fundamental measurement properties, and when they want to obtain estimates of item and person locations on a latent variable that reflect differences in item slopes. In addition, researchers choose the GPCM for rating scale analysis when they wish to evaluate category ordering and category precision specific to each item in their scale.

The equation for the GPCM is similar to the equation for the Partial Credit Model (see Chapter 3). The difference is that the GPCM includes an item-specific slope parameter (α_i). Specifically, the GPCM expresses the probability for a rating in a given rating scale category (category k) as:

$$P_{ni(x=k)} = \frac{\exp\left(\sum_{k=0}^{x} [\alpha_i(\theta_n - \delta_{ik})] \right)}{\sum_{j=0}^{m} \sum_{k=0}^{j} [\alpha_i(\theta_n - \delta_{ik})]} \tag{4.1}$$

Values of α_i can range from negative to positive infinity, where larger absolute values of α_i indicate that items discriminate more strongly among participants with different locations on the latent variable. When the slope parameter is positive, the probability for a response in a given category increases as participant locations increase. When the item slope is negative, participants with higher abilities have a lower probability for a response in higher rating scale categories compared to participants with lower abilities. If the slope parameter is close to zero, participants are likely to provide similar responses to the item, regardless of their location on the latent variable.

With the GPCM, person location estimates (θ) reflect person locations on a linear scale that represents the latent variable. For example, in the CES-D scale, person location estimates from the GPCM reflect the severity level of each participant's depression, based on their responses to the survey items. Lower values of theta indicate less-severe depression and higher values of theta represent more-severe depression.

Like the other models that we have considered in this book, item difficulty parameters for the GPCM (δ_i) reflect the level of the construct required for participants to provide positive responses to an item. In the CES-D scale, item difficulty reflects the level of depression required for participants to report that they have frequently felt or behaved as described in the item stems. For example, higher levels of depression may be required to respond *Most or all of the time* to Item 9: *I thought my life had been a failure* than for Item 15: *People were unfriendly*.

In the GPCM, item locations (i.e., item difficulty) are combined with threshold locations in the item-threshold parameter: δ_{ik}. As in the RSM and PCM, threshold parameters reflect the level of the construct (e.g., level of depression) required to provide a rating in a given category (e.g., *Most or all of the time*) rather than the category below it (e.g., *Occasionally or a moderate amount of time*). Specifically, the threshold estimate is the location on the logit scale at which there is an equal probability for a response in a given rating scale category (category k) and a response in the category below it (category $k - 1$). The number of thresholds is equal to one less than the number of categories. For example, three thresholds are calculated for each item with the four-category CES-D rating scale. Researchers can use these results to examine a variety of psychometric properties, including rating scale functioning.

Illustration of Rating Scale Analysis With the
Generalized Partial Credit Model

The GPCM allows analysts to evaluate rating scales for evidence of rating scale category ordering and rating scale category precision (see Table 4.1). In this section, the example CES-D scale data (see Chapter 1) are used to illustrate rating scale analysis with the GPCM. Table 4.2

Table 4.2 Rating Scale Category Calibrations From the GPCM (Selected Items)

Item	Rating Scale Category	% of Ratings	Average Participant Location Estimate (θ)	Threshold Estimate δ_{ik}	SE	Absolute Distance Between Adjacent Threshold Estimates
1	0	30%	−0.54	NA	NA	NA
	1	40%	−0.08	−0.77	0.08	NA
	2	26%	0.50	1.04	0.11	1.82
	3	4%	1.32	4.37	0.21	3.33
2	0	50%	−0.55	NA	NA	NA
	1	25%	0.16	0.88	0.08	NA
	2	17%	0.80	0.91	0.12	0.03
	3	8%	1.12	1.85	0.18	0.93
3	0	60%	−0.45	NA	NA	NA
	1	17%	0.26	1.71	0.08	NA
	2	13%	0.61	0.84[a]	0.12	0.87
	3	10%	1.37	1.20	0.18	0.36
6	0	51%	−0.50	NA	NA	NA
	1	25%	0.11	0.89	0.08	NA
	2	16%	0.75	1.00	0.12	0.11
	3	7%	1.29	2.05	0.19	1.05
9	0	56%	−0.43	NA	NA	NA
	1	22%	0.22	1.64	0.08	NA
	2	13%	0.61	1.27[a]	0.12	0.38
	3	9%	1.13	1.39	0.17	0.12
12	0	32%	−0.43	NA	NA	NA
	1	29%	−0.01	0.35	0.08	NA
	2	28%	0.25	0.18[a]	0.10	0.17
	3	11%	0.55	3.77	0.15	3.59
17	0	64%	−0.38	NA	NA	NA
	1	12%	0.27	3.12	0.08	NA
	2	12%	0.65	0.46[a]	0.12	2.65
	3	12%	1.06	0.73	0.17	0.27

[a]Disordered threshold.
Note: The Appendix includes results for all CES-D scale items.

provides a summary of numeric results from the GPCM rating scale analysis for selected items; Table A.4.1 in the Appendix for this chapter includes results for all items. Likewise, when indices involve graphical displays, results are shown for selected items for the sake of brevity. In practice, one would examine all of the indices for all of the items in an analysis.

All of the GPCM analyses were conducted using the Test Analysis Modules (TAM) package for R (Robitzsch et al., 2020). TAM is a package for the R software program that allows researchers to conduct many different types of psychometric analyses, including several IRT models. Details about getting started with R and annotated code for conducting the GPCM analyses using TAM is provided in the online supplement at **https://study.sagepub.com/researchmethods/qass/wind-exploring-rating-scale-functioning**.

Using TAM, the GPCM was estimated using the default Marginal Maximum Likelihood Estimation (MMLE) procedure. MMLE is an iterative process in which response probabilities in participant responses are used to identify estimates on a linear scale that represents a construct. For an introduction to estimation procedures using MMLE, please see DeAyala (2009).

Overall Model Results

When analysts apply the GPCM, they often examine indicators of overall fit between the data and the model (i.e., global model fit) before interpreting item-level and person-level results. In some cases, researchers may compare model fit between several candidate models, including the GPCM. For example, researchers may compare the fit of the GPCM to the fit of the PCM to choose the model that represents their data most accurately. For the CES-D scale data, there was a statistically significant difference in model fit between the GPCM and the PCM based on a likelihood ratio test between the two models. This model fit comparison test suggested that the GPCM provided a better representation of the data compared to the PCM, and this difference was statistically significant ($\chi^2(19) = 132.53$, $p < 0.01$). Some researchers may also consider differences in statistical model information, such as the Akaike Information Criteria (AIC) and Bayesian Information Criteria (BIC) values. These values reflect the "goodness of fit" for statistical models, taking into account the complexity of the model. In comparisons between models, researchers interpret lower values of AIC and BIC as

94

indicators of better model fit. The GPCM had lower AIC and BIC values (AIC = 37963.67; BIC = 38342.24) compared to the PCM (AIC = 38058.20; BIC = 38346.86). These model comparison results are not surprising, given that the GPCM incorporates additional information about the item responses through the discrimination parameter, and thus provides a more descriptive summary of the item responses.

When researchers conduct global model fit comparisons, they generally do so for the purpose of identifying the model that best represents the characteristics of their data. The guiding perspective in this book is that the choice of a model for rating scale analysis should be primarily informed and driven by the goals or research questions for that analysis. When researchers use statistical hypothesis tests to select a model that best represents their data, this is usually a different goal than selecting a model that will provide the most relevant details about rating scale functioning. In this chapter, we will focus on the types of information that the GPCM can provide about rating scale functioning. We revisit the idea of choosing between models for rating scale analysis in Chapter 6.

Some researchers who use the GPCM also examine item-level fit statistics. Specifically, some researchers conduct chi-square tests of conditional independence between each pair of items included in the analysis (Chen & Thissen, 1997). These tests evaluate whether participant responses to each item are statistically independent from all of the other items (i.e., local independence, see Chapter 2). This technique results in many chi-square statistics because it is applied to every pair of items in the analysis. For the CES-D items, there were 190 chi-square tests of conditional independence between each of the 20 items and the other items in the scale. Holm-adjusted p-values for these tests that take into account multiple statistical tests were not significant at $p < 0.01$. This result provides support for the use of the GPCM to analyze the CES-D scale data. For more details about these statistics in the context of the GPCM, please see Muraki and Muraki (2018).

Next, analysts may examine item-level psychometric properties, including overall item difficulty estimates and item discrimination parameters. Table 4.3 shows the overall item location estimates (δ_i) as well as item discrimination parameters (α_i), as calculated using the GPCM. With the default settings in the TAM package, the item location estimates were not centered at zero logits, as is sometimes done in IRT procedures. The average item location parameter was $\delta = 1.35$ (SD = 0.13). The item discrimination parameters ($M_\alpha = 0.58$, $SD_\alpha = 0.14$) ranged from $\alpha = 0.27$ for the reverse-coded version of Item 12 (*I was happy*), which was the least discriminating item, to $\alpha = 0.81$ for

Table 4.3 Overall Item Estimates From the GPCM

Item Number	Discrimination	Overall Location
1	0.51	1.55
2	0.69	1.21
3	0.69	1.25
4	0.48	1.38
5	0.81	1.26
6	0.68	1.31
7	0.70	1.14
8	0.43	1.12
9	0.54	1.44
10	0.66	1.34
11	0.58	1.32
12	0.27	1.43
13	0.60	1.56
14	0.72	1.28
15	0.51	1.55
16	0.30	1.55
17	0.52	1.44
18	0.69	1.35
19	0.62	1.30
20	0.66	1.26

Item 5 (*I had trouble keeping my mind on what I was doing*), which was the most discriminating item. Overall, the item discrimination results indicate that there were some differences in the degree to which the CES-D items discriminated among participants related to their level of depression. Some items, such as Item 12, did not distinguish much among participants while others, such as Item 5, were more discriminating.

With regard to item difficulty, the reverse-coded version of Item 8 (*I felt hopeful about the future*) had the lowest overall location (δ = 1.12). This means that participants were likely to indicate that they frequently felt or behaved in the way described in this item regardless of their level of depression. Item 13 (*I talked less than usual*) had the

96

highest overall location ($\delta = 1.56$); relatively severe levels of depression were required for participants to provide a high rating for this item. Participant locations (θ) ranged from $-6.12 \le \theta \le 3.78$ logits, with an average location of $\theta = -0.01$ logits (SD = 1.18).

Next, we will examine results from the rating scale analyses based on the GPCM as they relate to rating scale category ordering and rating scale category precision. The purpose, interpretation, and use of these indicators is similar to their use with polytomous Rasch models, as discussed in Chapter 3.

Rating Scale Category Ordering

Like their use in rating scale analysis with polytomous Rasch models (see Chapter 3), rating scale category ordering indicators for the GPCM help researchers evaluate whether rating scale categories can be interpreted in the intended order. For example, in the CES-D scale, rating scale category ordering helps analysts evaluate the degree to which responses in increasing categories reflect increasing levels of depression. We will use the same three rating scale category ordering indicators as we did in Chapter 3: Average participant locations within rating scale categories, logit-scale location estimates of rating scale category thresholds, and ordering of category probability curves.

Average Participant Locations Within Rating Scale Categories

First, researchers can examine the average participant location on the latent variable (mean theta; M_θ), as estimated using the GPCM, within each rating scale category. If rating scale categories are ordered as expected, the average participant location on the theta scale should increase as categories increase along the ordinal rating scale. When average participant locations correspond to the expected category order, this is evidence that higher categories reflect higher levels of the construct. For example, in the CES-D scale, we should see that participants with higher levels of depression (higher theta estimates) tend to respond in higher categories compared to participants with lower levels of depression (lower theta estimates).

Table 4.2 shows the average participant location estimates on the theta scale from the GPCM for participants who responded in each rating scale category in the example CES-D scale data. These values are the average participant location estimate from the GPCM among participants who provided a rating in each category of the rating scale, specific to each item. For example, for Item 1, participants who responded in category 0 had an average location of $M_{\theta,0} = -0.54$, which was lower than the average location for participants who responded in category 1 ($M_{\theta,1} = -0.08$), category 2 ($M_{\theta,2} = 0.50$), and category 3 ($M_{\theta,3} = 1.32$). The average participant locations reflected the intended category order ($M_{\theta,0} \leq M_{\theta,1} \leq M_{\theta,2} \leq M_{\theta,3}$) for all items in the CES-D scale. This result suggests that, on average, participants with higher levels of depression selected higher rating scale categories within each item. This result provides one piece of evidence that the CES-D rating scale was oriented in the expected direction.

Logit-Scale Location Estimates of Item-Specific Rating Scale Category Thresholds

A second technique for evaluating category ordering with the GPCM is to examine the location of rating scale category thresholds for each item. As in the RSM and PCM, category thresholds for the GPCM reflect the intersection points between categories. These values are represented using δ_{ik} in the GPCM equation (Equation 4.1). When the threshold locations are ordered as expected, lower levels of the latent variable (e.g., less severe depression) are required to respond in lower categories of the rating scale, and higher levels of the latent variable (e.g., more severe depression) are required to provide ratings in higher categories. In other words, the thresholds should match the expected order given the orientation of the rating scale. In the context of the CES-D scale, which has three thresholds (δ_{i1}, δ_{i2}, δ_{i3}), these values should be ordered such that $\delta_{i1} < \delta_{i2} < \delta_{i3}$.

Table 4.2 shows item-specific threshold location estimates from the GPCM. The threshold estimates for the CES-D scale data indicate rating scale category disordering for several items (Items 3, 4, 8, 9, 10, 11, 12, 13, 14, 16, 17, 19), as marked using asterisks in Table 4.2. For these items, there was a mismatch between the intended category order and the observed order in the data. In other words, higher levels of depression were not always required to provide higher ratings on more than half of the CES-D items. For example, for Item 3, the first two threshold values were not ordered as expected, because δ_{i2}, which represents the location at which there is an equal probability for a rating in category 1 and category 2, was located *lower* on the logit scale (0.84 logits) compared to δ_{i1} (1.71 logits), which represents the location at which there is an equal probability for a rating in category 0 and category 1. Practically speaking, this means that higher levels of depression were required to respond in category 1 compared to category 2, which is not in line with the intended orientation of the CES-D rating scale. This result suggests that the level of depression required to respond in each rating scale category did not always correspond to the intended order, and that category ordering varied across items.

Ordering of Item-Specific Category Probability Curves

Finally, as with polytomous Rasch models, researchers can use graphical displays of category probabilities to evaluate rating scale category ordering with the GPCM. These plots have the same interpretation as the category probability curves that we examined in Chapters 2 and 3: The x-axis shows estimates of participant locations, and separate lines show the conditional probability for a rating in each category. The points at which the category curves intersect correspond to the thresholds. When categories are ordered as expected, participants with low locations on the latent variable (e.g., less severe depression) should be most likely to respond in lower categories, and participants with high locations (e.g., more severe depression) should be most likely to respond in higher categories.

Figure 4.2 shows plots of category probability curves from the GPCM for selected items that had different patterns of category ordering. For example, the plots for Item 1 and Item 15 show category probability curves that are ordered as expected. The probabilities for each category increase and decrease successively as the logit scale moves from low to high. In the context of the CES-D scale, this means that the lower categories correspond to lower levels of depression and higher categories correspond to higher levels of depression.

In contrast, the plots for Item 3 and Item 11 show *dis*ordered rating scale category thresholds. For Item 3, the threshold (intersection point) between the first and second categories ($x = 0$ and $x = 1$) is *higher* on the logit scale than the threshold between the second and third categories ($x = 1$ and $x = 2$). Likewise, for Item 11, the threshold between the second and third categories ($x = 1$ and $x = 2$) is *higher* on the logit scale than the threshold between the third and fourth categories ($x = 2$ and $x = 3$). These results suggest that the CES-D rating scale categories may not be ordered as expected for some items, and that category ordering varies across items—potentially compromising the interpretation of the scale. We will explore these results in more detail in the next section as we consider category precision indicators.

As we saw with the PCM in Chapter 3, it is interesting to note that conclusions about category ordering from the perspective of rating scale category thresholds and graphical displays of category probabilities were different from the conclusions based on average participant locations within categories. These indices provide different perspectives on category ordering that are not always perfectly aligned. Evidence of category disordering based on any indicator suggests that participants may not have interpreted the rating scale categories in the intended order, and that additional investigation and consideration is warranted.

Rating Scale Category Precision

As we saw in Chapter 3, rating scale category precision refers to the degree to which each category in a rating scale can identify participants who have meaningfully different locations on the latent variable. When rating scale categories are precise, they describe a range of locations on the latent variable (e.g., a range of depression levels) that is distinct from another rating scale category. The GPCM provides several indicators that researchers can use to evaluate rating scale category precision: the distance between threshold location estimates on the logit scale and category probability curves.

Distance Between Item-Specific Threshold Location Estimates on the Logit Scale

One indicator of rating scale category precision is the range of participant locations on the logit scale within which participants are most likely to respond in each category. To evaluate this, we can calculate the distance on the logit scale between thresholds for adjacent categories as we did for the Rasch models in Chapter 3. The general interpretation of these distances is similar between Rasch models and the GPCM: larger distances indicate that a category reflects a wider range of the latent variable, and smaller distances indicate that a category reflects a narrow range of the latent variable. In general, these distances should be large enough to identify participants with meaningful differences on the latent variable but also small enough to provide appropriate distinction among participants.

Whereas there is some guidance on how to interpret these distances for Rasch models (see Figure 3.1), researchers have not presented critical values with which to evaluate these distances based on the GPCM. Nonetheless, analysts can evaluate the distances between

100

adjacent threshold estimates in light of the purpose of a measurement procedure. Some situations may warrant fewer rating scale categories that each describe a relatively wide range of locations on the latent variable, and others may warrant more rating scale categories that each describe a small range of locations.

Table 4.2 shows the absolute distance between adjacent threshold estimates for the CES-D scale based on the GPCM. These values show the distance between adjacent rating scale categories on the same metric that we have used to describe person locations and item locations. Larger distances indicate that there is a more substantial difference in the severity of depression between two categories, and smaller distances indicate that the difference is smaller. For the CES-D scale items, these distances range from 0.03 logits between the first two thresholds for Item 2 to 2.59 logits between the second and third thresholds for Item 12. Looking across the CES-D items, there are notably small distances between the first two thresholds ($|(\delta_{i2} - \delta_{i1})| \leq 0.3$) for several items (Items 2, 6, 7, 12, and 13); these values suggest that the middle rating scale categories may not discern meaningful differences among participants. In addition, for Item 9 and Item 17, the distance between the second and third thresholds was also quite small ($|(\delta_{i3} - \delta_{i2})| \leq 0.27$). In light of both of these results, researchers may consider adjusting the scale length or revising rating scale category labels or descriptions in future administrations of the CES-D. Because some of the categories reflect very narrow ranges, fewer categories may be sufficient for this instrument.

Distinct Item-Specific Category Probability Curves

Similar to the models discussed in Chapters 2 and 3, researchers can examine plots of rating scale category probabilities (Figure 4.1) for evidence that each category describes a unique range of participant locations on the latent variable. When rating scale categories are precise, the curve associated with each category has a unique range of locations on the logit scale at which it is most probable.

Returning to Figure 4.2, we will now consider the CES-D rating scale category probability curves from the perspective of category precision. The curves for Item 1 and Item 15 indicate that all four rating scale categories have a distinct range on the latent variable at which they are the most probable. These plots indicate that the rating scale categories reflect distinct ranges on the logit scale. On the other hand, the category probability curves for Item 3 and Item 11 clearly indicate that one or

Figure 4.2 Plots of Category Probabilities for Selected CES-D Items Based on the Generalized Partial Credit Model

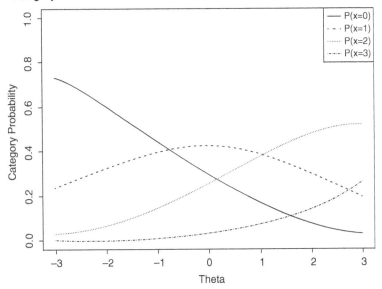

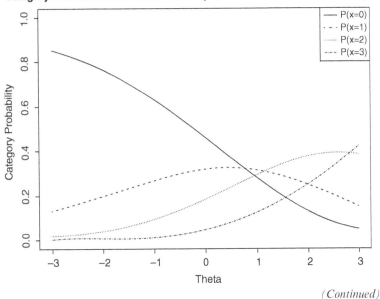

(Continued)

Figure 4.2 Plots of Category Probabilities for Selected CES-D Items Based on the Generalized Partial Credit Model *(Continued)*

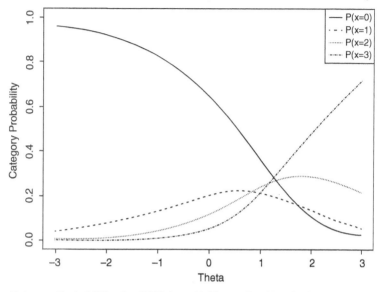

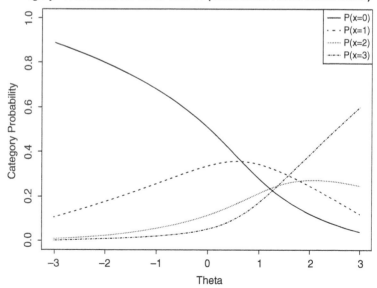

both of the middle categories ($x = 1$ and $x = 2$) do not have a distinct range on the logit scale at which they are more probable than the other categories. This result provides further evidence that the middle categories for the CES-D rating scale are not providing distinct information about participants' depression levels.

Rating Scale Analysis Using Polytomous IRT
Models With a Cumulative Probability Formulation

The second category of models for this chapter is polytomous IRT models that use a *cumulative probability* formulation. To understand the nature of cumulative probability IRT models, it is useful to compare them to the models discussed so far in this book. The RSM, PCM, and GPCM are *adjacent categories* models. This means that rating scale category thresholds are calculated using the probability of a response in a given category, rather than in the category just below it ($P(x = k)/P(x = k - 1)$). For example, for a four-category ordinal rating scale ($x = 0, 1, 2, 3$), rating scale category thresholds are modeled as three dichotomies:

- Category 1 versus Category 0: $x = 1$ versus $x = 0$
- Category 2 versus Category 1: $x = 2$ versus $x = 1$
- Category 3 versus Category 2: $x = 3$ versus $x = 2$.

In contrast, cumulative probability IRT models model the probability for a rating in a given category *or any higher category* ($P(x \geq k)/P(x < k)$). In a rating scale with four ordered categories, such as the CES-D scale, the cumulative probabilities would be modeled using the following comparisons:

- Category 1 or higher: $x \geq 1$ versus $x < 1$
- Category 2 or higher: $x \geq 2$ versus $x < 2$
- Category 3 or higher: $x \geq 3$ versus $x < 3$.

In cumulative models, the cumulative probability associated with the lowest category ($x \geq 0$) is equal to 1.00 by definition. The major practical implication of the cumulative probability formulation is that rating scale categories are always ordered as expected. Researchers may select cumulative probability models when they do not need information about category ordering or disordering for their analyses.

Graded Response Model

The Graded Response Model (GRM; Samejima, 1969, 2018)[1] is a polytomous IRT model with a cumulative probability formulation that can be used to model ordinal item response data that are scored in three or more categories.

In the equation for GRM, item locations are combined with threshold locations as an *item-category* parameter: δ_{ik}. These values are defined as the location on the logit scale at which there is an equal probability for a response in a given rating scale category *or any higher category*. For example, in the four-category CES-D scale, there are three item-category parameters for each item (δ_{i1}, δ_{i2}, δ_{i3}) that are interpreted as follows:

- δ_{i1} = The location where there is an equal probability for a response in category 1 and any category greater than 1

- δ_{i2} = The location where there is an equal probability for a response in category 2 and any category greater than 2

- δ_{i3} = The location where there is an equal probability for a response in category 3 and any category greater than 3

Each category probability can be represented using a unique equation. For the lowest category in the scale (category $k = 0$), the probability is:

$$P_{ni(x=0)} = 1 - \frac{\exp[\alpha_i(\theta_n - \delta_{ik})]}{1 + \exp[\alpha_i(\theta_n - \delta_{ik})]} \qquad (4.2)$$

For each of the categories between 1 and the highest category in the scale ($0 < k < m$), the probability is:

$$P_{ni(x=k)} = \frac{\exp[\alpha_i(\theta_n - \delta_{ik})]}{1 + \exp[\alpha_i(\theta_n - \delta_{ik})]} - \frac{\exp[\alpha_i(\theta_n - \delta_{ik+1})]}{1 + \exp[\alpha_i(\theta_n - \delta_{ik+1})]} \qquad (4.3)$$

---

[1]There are several variations on the GRM that appear in the literature. In this volume, we focus on the homogeneous version of the GRM, where the discrimination parameter is constant within an item. This model is relatively simpler than other versions of the GRM and it can be applied in many survey research contexts.

For the highest category in the scale ($k = m$), the probability is:

$$P_{ni(x=k)} = \frac{\exp[\alpha_i(\theta_n - \delta_{ik})]}{1 + \exp[\alpha_i(\theta_n - \delta_{ik})]} \quad (4.4)$$

The GRM provides analysts with estimates of participant locations (θ) on the latent variable, item-specific cumulative threshold locations (δ_{ik}), and item-specific discrimination (α_i). To illustrate the threshold interpretation for the GRM, Figure 4.3 shows plots of cumulative category probabilities for Item 15 from the CES-D scale, as calculated using the GRM. The x-axis shows the theta scale, and the y-axis shows cumulative category probabilities. Separate lines reflect the three probabilities that are modeled in the GRM: $P(x \geq 1)$, $P(x \geq 2)$, and $P(x \geq 3)$. Vertical lines are used to show the thresholds (δ_{ik}), which are located at the point at which the cumulative probability equals 0.50 ($\delta_{11,1} = -3.64$, $\delta_{11,2} = -1.49$, and $\delta_{11,3} = 0.28$).

Figure 4.3 Plot of Cumulative Category Probabilities Based on the GRM

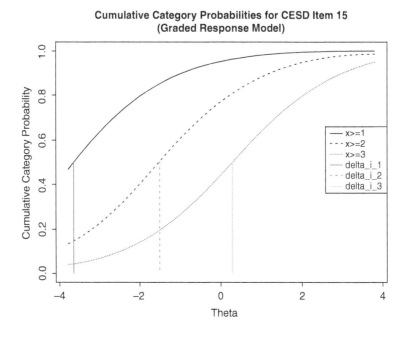

It is also possible to construct plots that show the probability associated with individual categories based on the GRM. These plots are different from the cumulative probabilities plots because they show the probability for a rating *in* each category (e.g., $x = 0$, $x = 1$, $x = 2$, and $x = 3$) rather than the probability for a rating *in or above* each category. To illustrate, Figure 4.4 shows a plot of category probabilities for Item 15 from the CES-D based on the GRM. The x-axis shows the logit scale, and the y-axis shows conditional category probabilities. The conditional probability for a rating in each category is shown using separate curved lines. Straight solid vertical lines show the mode for each category.

To illustrate the interpretation of category probability plots for the GRM, consider Figure 4.4. For the lowest and highest categories, the values of δ_{ij} indicate the logit scale location at which there is a 0.50 probability for a response in the category. In Figure 4.4, the location of the first threshold ($\delta_{11,1} = -3.64$ logits) corresponds to the point on the

Figure 4.4 Plot of Category Probabilities Based on the GRM for CES-D Scale Item 15

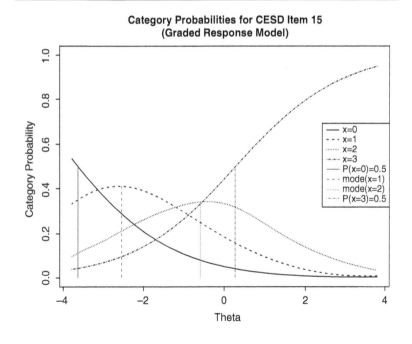

logit scale at which the probability for $x = 0$ is equal to 0.50. Likewise, the location of the third (and final) threshold ($\delta_{11,3} = 0.28$ logits) corresponds to the point which the probability for $x = 3$ is equal to 0.50. For the nonextreme categories ($0 < k < m$), the values of δ_{ij} specify the *mode* of the category response function, where $\text{mode}_{xk} = (\delta_{k+1} + \delta_k)/2$. This value is the logit-scale location at which a response in the given category is most probable. In Figure 4.4, the mode of the category response function for $x = 1$ is located at $((\delta_{11,2} + \delta_{11,1})/2) = ((-1.49 + -3.64)/2) = -2.57$ logits. The mode for $x = 2$ is located at $((\delta_{11,3} + \delta_{11,2})/2) = ((0.28 + -1.49)/2) = -0.61$ logits.

Illustration of Rating Scale Analysis With the Graded Response Model

In this section, the example CES-D scale data are used to illustrate rating scale analysis with the GRM. Table 4.4 provides a summary of numeric results from the GPCM rating scale analysis for selected items; Table A.4.2 in the Appendix for this chapter includes results

Table 4.4 Rating Scale Category Calibrations From the GRM (Selected Items)

Item	It Rating Scale Category	It% of Ratings	It Average Participant Location Within Category	Threshold Estimate δ_{ik}	SE	It Absolute Distance Between Adjacent Threshold Estimates
1	0	30%	−1.14	NA	NA	NA
	1	40%	−0.42	−4.66	0.52	NA
	2	26%	0.07	−1.24	0.27	3.41
	3	4%	0.34	1.29	0.27	2.53
12	0	32%	−0.47	NA	NA	NA
	1	29%	−0.22	−4.54	0.70	NA
	2	28%	0.02	−1.00	0.25	3.55
	3	11%	0.25	1.58	0.35	2.58
13	0	44%	−0.97	NA	NA	NA
	1	27%	−0.60	−3.69	0.34	NA
	2	24%	0.00	−1.13	0.21	2.56
	3	5%	0.36	0.31	0.17	1.44

(Continued)

Table 4.4 Rating Scale Category Calibrations From the GRM (Selected Items) *(Continued)*

Item	*It Rating Scale Category*	*It% of Ratings*	*It Average Participant Location Within Category*	*Threshold Estimate* δ_{ik}	*SE*	*It Absolute Distance Between Adjacent Threshold Estimates*
14	0	55%	−1.08	NA	NA	NA
	1	20%	−0.66	−2.48	0.19	NA
	2	17%	−0.20	−1.14	0.16	1.35
	3	8%	0.38	−0.20	0.11	0.94
15	0	45%	−0.88	NA	NA	NA
	1	29%	−0.53	−3.64	0.37	NA
	2	19%	−0.05	−1.49	0.24	2.15
	3	6%	0.32	0.28	0.16	1.78
17	0	64%	−0.90	NA	NA	NA
	1	12%	−0.55	−2.29	0.20	NA
	2	12%	−0.26	−1.37	0.19	0.93
	3	12%	0.27	−0.67	0.13	0.69
20	0	45%	−1.10	NA	NA	NA
	1	32%	−0.56	−2.86	0.24	NA
	2	16%	−0.12	−1.39	0.19	1.48
	3	7%	0.40	0.25	0.12	1.64

Note: The Appendix includes results for all CES-D scale items.

for all items. Likewise, when indices involve graphical displays, results are shown for selected items for the sake of brevity. In practice, one would examine all of the indices for all of the items in an analysis.

All of the analyses were conducted using the "latent trait models" (ltm) package for R (Rizopoulos, 2006). The ltm package is a package for the R statistical software program that includes functions for several IRT models, including the GRM. Details about getting started with R and annotated code for conducting these analyses using ltm is provided in the online supplement at **https://study.sagepub.com/researchmethods/ qass/wind-exploring-rating-scale-functioning**.

Overall Model Results

When analysts apply the GRM, they often examine indicators of overall fit between the data and the model (i.e., global model fit) before interpreting item-level and person-level results.

In some cases, researchers may also compare model fit between several candidate models, including the GRM, in order to choose the model that represents the data most accurately. The considerations related to global model fit analyses and comparisons in the context of rating scale analysis that we discussed for the GPCM also apply to the GPCM. In addition, because the GRM has a different threshold formulation than the other models in this book, it is not straightforward to use a model comparison test as we did between the PCM and GPCM.

Item-level fit analysis can be conducted for the GRM by comparing observed and expected responses for pairs of variables (items). Large residuals indicate that the observed responses are meaningfully different from those that would be expected given the GRM. The ltm package flags pairs of items with statistically significant chi-square statistics. In the CES-D scale data, none of the item pairs were flagged for misfit using this approach.

Next, analysts may examine item-level psychometric properties, including overall item difficulty estimates and item discrimination parameters. Table 4.5 shows the overall item location estimates (δ_i) as well as item discrimination parameters (α_i). The average item location parameter was -1.36 logits (SD $= 0.14$). Item 15 (*People were unfriendly*) had the lowest overall location (-1.62 logits); participants tended to agree with this item even if they had low levels of depression. The reverse-coded version of Item 8 (*I felt hopeful about the future*) had the highest overall location (-1.08 logits); a relatively high level of depression was required for participants to report that they frequently felt or behaved as described in this item stem. The item discrimination parameters ($M = 0.97$, SD $= 0.22$) ranged from 0.48 for the reverse-coded version of Item 12 (*I was happy*), which was the least discriminating item, to 1.26 for Item 5 (*I had trouble keeping my mind on what I was doing*), which was the most discriminating item. Overall, the item discrimination results indicate that there were some differences in the degree to which the CES-D items discriminated between participants related to their level of depression. Participant locations (θ_n) ranged from -3.06 logits to 2.25 logits, with an average location of -0.03 logits (SD $= 0.89$).

110

Table 4.5 Overall Item Estimates From the GRM

Item Number	Discrimination	Overall Location
1	0.74	−1.54
2	1.15	−1.24
3	1.26	−1.26
4	0.86	−1.40
5	1.22	−1.21
6	1.09	−1.37
7	1.15	−1.16
8	0.79	−1.08
9	0.95	−1.53
10	1.10	−1.34
11	0.97	−1.46
12	0.48	−1.32
13	0.94	−1.50
14	1.24	−1.27
15	0.81	−1.62
16	0.52	−1.52
17	1.06	−1.44
18	1.03	−1.45
19	1.07	−1.29
20	1.05	−1.34

Rating Scale Category Ordering

Compared to IRT models that use the adjacent-categories probability formulation, models that use cumulative probability formulations, including the GRM, provide relatively limited information about rating scale category ordering (Andrich, 2015; Mellenbergh, 1995). Because of the cumulative probability formulation, the item-specific thresholds for the GRM are always ordered as expected. Demonstrating this property, Table 4.4 shows the item-threshold locations for selected CES-D items based on the GRM. For all items in the CES-D scale, the threshold values increased as the categories progressed along the ordinal rating scale. As a result, it is not meaningful to examine threshold parameters as evidence of category ordering with the GRM. Nonetheless, analysts can evaluate the general orientation of the rating scale categories with the latent variable by examining the average participant location estimates on the theta scale (θ) within rating scale categories for individual items.

Average Participant Locations Within Item-Specific Rating Scale Categories for Individual Items

Although the GRM uses a cumulative probability formulation, analysts can evaluate rating scale category ordering by examining the average participant location estimate on the theta scale (θ) within rating scale categories specific to individual items. These results are interpreted in the same way as they were for the models discussed so far in this book. If the rating scale is oriented in the correct direction, we expect to see increasing average participant locations as categories progress from low to high on the rating scale.

Table 4.4 shows the average participant location estimates from the GRM within rating scale categories for selected CES-D items. We can see that the average participant locations increase across increasing rating scale categories for all items in the CES-D. This result provides support for interpreting higher rating scale categories as indicators of higher levels of depression for all items in the CES-D.

Rating Scale Category Precision

It is also possible to examine GRM results for evidence of rating scale category precision. As we have seen for the other models in this book, rating scale category precision indices help analysts evaluate the degree to which individual categories in a rating scale provide unique information about differences among participants with regard to the latent variable. With the GRM, rating scale category precision can be evaluated by examining the distance between rating scale category threshold estimates on the logit scale for individual items, and plots of cumulative category probabilities for individual items.

Distance Between Rating Scale Category Threshold Estimates on the Logit Scale for Individual Items

The absolute value of the difference between item-specific rating scale category threshold estimates calculated using the GRM ($|(\delta_{ik} - \delta_{ik-1})|$) describes the degree to which each category provides unique information about the latent variable. Larger absolute distances indicate that

112

each successive category provided unique information about participants with regard to the latent variable. Similar to the GPCM, researchers have not established critical values or guidelines for evaluating these distances for the GRM. As a result, analysts should consider these values with respect to the level of granularity that is needed to make meaningful distinctions among participants. Whereas some assessment contexts may require more nuanced differentiation among participants, others may warrant fewer categories that describe a larger range of locations on the latent variable.

For the CES-D scale data, the absolute value of the distance between thresholds ranged from 0.69 logits between the second and third threshold for Item 17 to 3.55 logits between the first and second threshold for Item 12. These values suggest that, when modeled using cumulative probabilities, there is a distinct range on the latent variable associated with each set of successive rating scale categories. From the perspective of GRM, the CES-D rating scale categories provide distinct information about participants' levels of depression.

Plots of Cumulative Category Probabilities for Individual Items

As another indicator of rating scale category precision, one can examine plots of cumulative category probabilities for each item. For rating scales with categories $x = 0, 1, \ldots, m$, these plots show the probability for a rating in or above categories 1 through m. For example, in the CES-D scale, cumulative category probability plots show the probability for a rating in or above the second, third, and fourth rating scale categories.

When rating scale categories provide unique information, these curves are distinct and do not overlap. Large distances between cumulative category probabilities suggest that rating scale categories reflect substantial differences in the latent variable. On the other hand, cumulative category probabilities that overlap suggest that the rating scale categories may be redundant—that is, fewer categories may be sufficient to differentiate among participants' locations on the latent variable.

Figure 4.5 shows plots of cumulative category probabilities for selected CES-D scale items, calculated using the GRM. Person locations on the theta scale are plotted along the x-axis, and the probability for a rating in category k or higher is plotted along the y-axis. Separate lines show the probabilities associated with a rating in category 1 or higher, category 2 or higher, and category 3 or higher. Vertical lines are plotted to show the location of the δ_{ik} values on the logit scale.

Figure 4.5 Plots of Cumulative Category Probabilities for Selected CES-D Items Based on the GRM

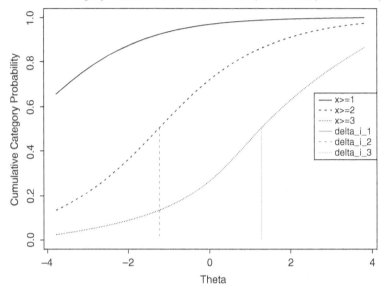

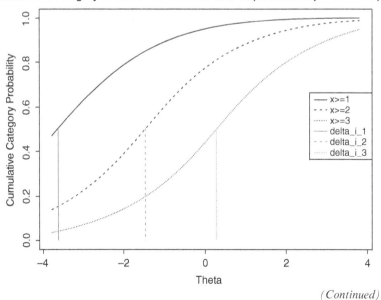

(Continued)

Figure 4.5 Plots of Cumulative Category Probabilities for Selected CES-D Items Based on the GRM *(Continued)*

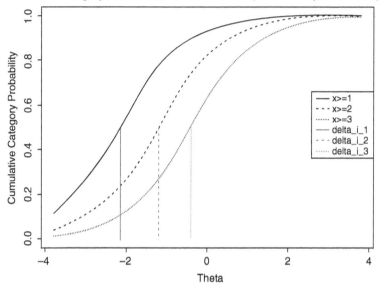

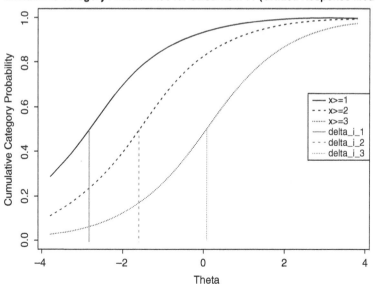

Figure 4.6 Plots of Individual Category Probabilities for Selected CES-D Items Based on the GRM

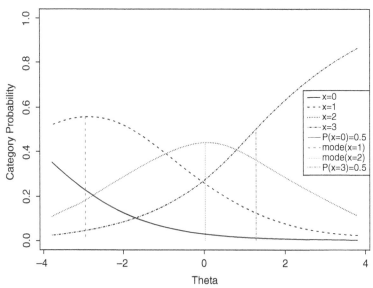

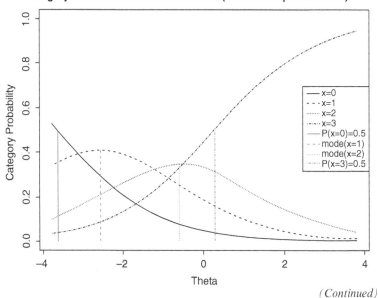

(Continued)

Figure 4.6 Plots of Individual Category Probabilities for Selected CES-D Items Based on the GRM *(Continued)*

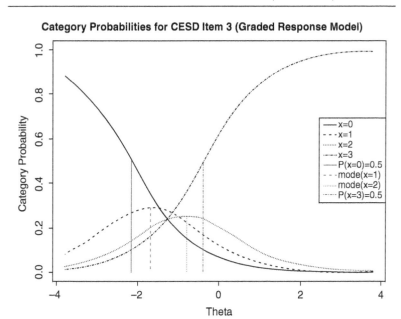

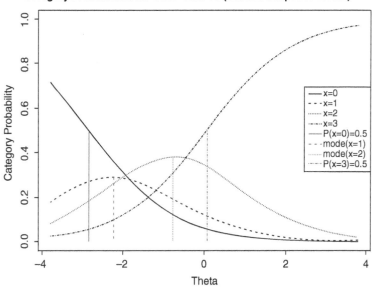

In the plots for Item 1, Item 15, and Item 11, the distance between adjacent cumulative category probabilities is relatively large. This means that there is a notable difference in the level of depression among participants who responded in or above category 0 or 1, category 2, and category 3. In addition, the difference in the level of depression needed for a rating in or above categories 1 and 2 was larger compared to the difference in the level of depression needed for a rating in or above category 2 and category 3 for each of these items. In contrast, the cumulative category probabilities for Item 3 are closer together. This means that the difference in the level of depression required to respond in or above category 1, category 2, and category 3 were relatively less distinct.

Plots of Individual Category Probabilities for Individual Items

It may also be useful to examine plots of individual rating scale category probabilities based on the GRM. Although these plots are not used to identify category disordering (as in the RSM, PCM, and GPCM), they provide insight into the distinctiveness of item-specific rating scale categories. Specifically, analysts can examine plots of GRM category probabilities to identify the degree to which each item-specific rating scale category describes a unique range of locations on the latent variable. In the context of the CES-D scale, distinct category probability curves indicate that each category in the rating scale reflects a level of depression that is distinct from the other categories.

The plots in Figure 4.6 show GRM individual category probabilities for four selected items from the CES-D scale. In the plots for Item 1 and Item 15, all four categories in the CES-D rating scale have a distinct mode. This means that there is a unique range of depression levels at which participants would be most likely to select each category. However, in the plots for Item 3 and Item 11, one or more categories does not have a distinct mode. Nonmodal categories suggest that for these items, the rating scale categories do not provide unique information about participants' depression levels. This result suggests that fewer categories may be sufficient for describing levels of depression.

Chapter Summary

This chapter provided an overview of two types of parametric non-Rasch models that researchers can use to gather information about rating scale functioning: (1) polytomous IRT models with slope parameters, and (2) polytomous IRT models with a cumulative probability formulation. We used the Generalized Partial Credit Model (GPCM) as an example of the former and the Graded Response Model (GRM) as an example of the latter. Both of these models provide information that can help researchers evaluate rating scale functioning for their survey data.

First, researchers can use the GPCM when they want to incorporate differences in item discrimination (i.e., item slope) into their parameter estimates. Because the GPCM includes item slopes in the equation, it usually has statistically better overall fit than models without slope parameters, such as the PCM, with some tradeoffs in the complexity of the model interpretation. An important feature of the GPCM is that, like the Rasch models discussed in Chapters 2 and 3, it can help researchers evaluate their survey data for evidence that the rating scale categories are ordered as expected. This information is provided for each item. The GPCM also provides information about rating scale category precision specific to each item. Researchers can use this information to evaluate whether individual categories in their rating scales describe unique levels of a latent variable, specific to each item.

The GRM is another popular IRT model that appears throughout survey research literature. In this chapter, we considered the GRM as an example of a polytomous IRT model that is based on *cumulative rating scale probabilities.* Practically, this means that the GRM does not allow rating scale category thresholds to be disordered. This model is useful in some modeling contexts where directly evaluating category ordering may not be needed. Nonetheless, researchers can still use the GRM to obtain a general sense of the orientation of their rating scales and to evaluate rating scale category precision.

Each of the models illustrated in this chapter provides unique information that can help researchers evaluate rating scale functioning for their surveys and identify areas and directions for revision. In the next chapter, we consider nonparametric models that can also provide insight into rating scale functioning.

APPENDIX

Table A.4.1 Rating Scale Category Calibrations From the GPCM: All CES-D Scale Items

Item	Rating Scale Category	% of Ratings	Average Participant Location Estimate (θ)	Threshold Estimate δ_{ik}	SE	Absolute Distance Between Adjacent Threshold Estimates
1	0	30%	−0.54	NA	NA	NA
	1	40%	−0.08	−0.77	0.08	NA
	2	26%	0.50	1.04	0.11	1.82
	3	4%	1.32	4.37	0.21	3.33
2	0	50%	−0.55	NA	NA	NA
	1	25%	0.16	0.88	0.08	NA
	2	17%	0.80	0.91	0.12	0.03
	3	8%	1.12	1.85	0.18	0.93
3	0	60%	−0.45	NA	NA	NA
	1	17%	0.26	1.71	0.08	NA
	2	13%	0.61	0.84[a]	0.12	0.87
	3	10%	1.37	1.20	0.18	0.36
4	0	51%	−0.46	NA	NA	NA
	1	22%	0.12	1.65	0.07	NA
	2	18%	0.57	0.68[a]	0.11	0.97
	3	10%	0.93	1.79	0.16	1.10
5	0	40%	−0.69	NA	NA	NA
	1	32%	0.08	0.04	0.08	NA
	2	24%	0.71	0.68	0.12	0.64
	3	4%	1.57	3.07	0.22	2.39
6	0	51%	−0.50	NA	NA	NA
	1	25%	0.11	0.89	0.08	NA
	2	16%	0.75	1.00	0.12	0.11
	3	7%	1.29	2.05	0.19	1.05
7	0	47%	−0.56	NA	NA	NA
	1	27%	0.13	0.66	0.08	NA
	2	17%	0.62	0.96	0.12	0.30

(Continued)

Table A.4.1 Rating Scale Category Calibrations From the GPCM: All CES-D Scale Items *(Continued)*

Item	Rating Scale Category	% of Ratings	Average Participant Location Estimate (θ)	Threshold Estimate δ_{ik}	SE	Absolute Distance Between Adjacent Threshold Estimates
	3	9%	1.33	1.79	0.18	0.83
8	0	44%	−0.50	NA	NA	NA
	1	21%	0.08	1.57	0.07	NA
	2	21%	0.37	0.16[a]	0.11	1.42
	3	13%	0.87	1.62	0.15	1.46
9	0	56%	−0.43	NA	NA	NA
	1	22%	0.22	1.64	0.08	NA
	2	13%	0.61	1.27[a]	0.12	0.38
	3	9%	1.13	1.39	0.17	0.12
10	0	53%	−0.50	NA	NA	NA
	1	22%	0.11	1.21	0.08	NA
	2	19%	0.75	0.57[a]	0.12	0.64
	3	7%	1.22	2.24	0.18	1.67
11	0	49%	−0.51	NA	NA	NA
	1	30%	0.17	0.71	0.07	NA
	2	13%	0.84	1.81	0.12	1.10
	3	9%	0.94	1.44[a]	0.18	0.37
12	0	32%	−0.43	NA	NA	NA
	1	29%	−0.01	0.35	0.08	NA
	2	28%	0.25	0.18[a]	0.10	0.17
	3	11%	0.55	3.77	0.15	3.59
13	0	44%	−0.52	NA	NA	NA
	1	27%	−0.01	0.66	0.08	NA
	2	24%	0.72	0.49[a]	0.11	0.17
	3	5%	1.13	3.54	0.21	3.05
14	0	55%	−0.52	NA	NA	NA
	1	20%	0.24	1.27	0.08	NA
	2	17%	0.77	0.60[a]	0.12	0.66

(Continued)

Table A.4.1 Rating Scale Category Calibrations From the GPCM: All CES-D Scale Items *(Continued)*

Item	Rating Scale Category	% of Ratings	Average Participant Location Estimate (θ)	Threshold Estimate δ_{ik}	SE	Absolute Distance Between Adjacent Threshold Estimates
	3	8%	1.27	1.97	0.18	1.37
15	0	45%	−0.46	NA	NA	NA
	1	29%	0.04	0.71	0.07	NA
	2	19%	0.62	1.14	0.11	0.43
	3	6%	1.05	2.81	0.18	1.66
16	0	37%	−0.38	NA	NA	NA
	1	27%	−0.10	0.95	0.07	NA
	2	25%	0.38	0.39[a]	0.10	0.56
	3	10%	0.60	3.32	0.16	2.93
17	0	64%	−0.38	NA	NA	NA
	1	12%	0.27	3.12	0.08	NA
	2	12%	0.65	0.46[a]	0.12	2.65
	3	12%	1.06	0.73	0.17	0.27
18	0	42%	−0.60	NA	NA	NA
	1	36%	0.16	0.04	0.08	NA
	2	17%	0.70	1.48	0.12	1.44
	3	5%	1.30	2.54	0.20	1.07
19	0	53%	−0.50	NA	NA	NA
	1	20%	0.18	1.48	0.08	NA
	2	18%	0.64	0.43[a]	0.12	1.05
	3	9%	1.19	1.97	0.17	1.54
20	0	45%	−0.57	NA	NA	NA
	1	32%	0.16	0.34	0.08	NA
	2	16%	0.67	1.44	0.12	1.09
	3	7%	1.27	2.00	0.17	0.56

[a]Disordered threshold.

Table A.4.2 Rating Scale Category Calibrations From the GRM: All CES-D Scale Items

Item	Rating Scale Category	% of Ratings	Average Participant Location Within Category	Threshold Estimate δ_{ik}	SE	Absolute Distance Between Adjacent Threshold Estimates
1	0	30%	−1.14	NA	NA	NA
	1	40%	−0.42	−4.66	0.52	NA
	2	26%	0.07	−1.24	0.27	3.41
	3	4%	0.34	1.29	0.27	2.53
2	0	50%	−0.96	NA	NA	NA
	1	25%	−0.68	−2.54	0.20	NA
	2	17%	−0.13	−1.19	0.17	1.36
	3	8%	0.40	0.01	0.11	1.20
3	0	60%	−1.22	NA	NA	NA
	1	17%	−0.51	−2.17	0.17	NA
	2	13%	−0.23	−1.21	0.16	0.96
	3	10%	0.33	−0.39	0.11	0.82
4	0	51%	−0.79	NA	NA	NA
	1	22%	−0.49	−2.88	0.28	NA
	2	18%	−0.11	−1.28	0.20	1.60
	3	10%	0.32	−0.03	0.12	1.25
5	0	40%	−1.38	NA	NA	NA
	1	32%	−0.61	−3.12	0.24	NA
	2	24%	−0.05	−0.95	0.18	2.16
	3	4%	0.49	0.45	0.15	1.40
6	0	51%	−1.10	NA	NA	NA
	1	25%	−0.65	−2.79	0.23	NA
	2	16%	−0.10	−1.30	0.19	1.49
	3	7%	0.37	−0.02	0.12	1.28
7	0	47%	−1.16	NA	NA	NA
	1	27%	−0.53	−2.48	0.20	NA
	2	17%	−0.11	−1.12	0.16	1.36
	3	9%	0.41	0.13	0.11	1.25

(Continued)

Table A.4.2 Rating Scale Category Calibrations From the GRM: All CES-D Scale Items *(Continued)*

Item	Rating Scale Category	% of Ratings	Average Participant Location Within Category	Threshold Estimate δ_{lk}	SE	Absolute Distance Between Adjacent Threshold Estimates
8	0	44%	−0.74	NA	NA	NA
	1	21%	−0.29	−2.64	0.28	NA
	2	21%	−0.07	−0.91	0.16	1.73
	3	13%	0.33	0.32	0.13	1.23
9	0	56%	−0.98	NA	NA	NA
	1	22%	−0.49	−2.77	0.26	NA
	2	13%	−0.18	−1.53	0.21	1.24
	3	9%	0.30	−0.29	0.13	1.24
10	0	53%	−1.06	NA	NA	NA
	1	22%	−0.63	−2.77	0.23	NA
	2	19%	−0.09	−1.16	0.18	1.61
	3	7%	0.36	−0.10	0.12	1.07
11	0	49%	−0.77	NA	NA	NA
	1	30%	−0.73	−2.84	0.25	NA
	2	13%	−0.16	−1.61	0.21	1.23
	3	9%	0.37	0.07	0.12	1.68
12	0	32%	−0.47	NA	NA	NA
	1	29%	−0.22	−4.54	0.70	NA
	2	28%	0.02	−1.00	0.25	3.55
	3	11%	0.25	1.58	0.35	2.58
13	0	44%	−0.97	NA	NA	NA
	1	27%	−0.60	−3.69	0.34	NA
	2	24%	0.00	−1.13	0.21	2.56
	3	5%	0.36	0.31	0.17	1.44
14	0	55%	−1.08	NA	NA	NA
	1	20%	−0.66	−2.48	0.19	NA
	2	17%	−0.20	−1.14	0.16	1.35
	3	8%	0.38	−0.20	0.11	0.94

(Continued)

Table A.4.2 Rating Scale Category Calibrations From the GRM: All CES-D Scale Items *(Continued)*

Item	Rating Scale Category	% of Ratings	Average Participant Location Within Category	Threshold Estimate δ_{ik}	SE	Absolute Distance Between Adjacent Threshold Estimates
15	0	45%	−0.88	NA	NA	NA
	1	29%	−0.53	−3.64	0.37	NA
	2	19%	−0.05	−1.49	0.24	2.15
	3	6%	0.32	0.28	0.16	1.78
16	0	37%	−0.50	NA	NA	NA
	1	27%	−0.31	−4.38	0.63	NA
	2	25%	0.07	−1.23	0.27	3.15
	3	10%	0.23	1.06	0.26	2.28
17	0	64%	−0.90	NA	NA	NA
	1	12%	−0.55	−2.29	0.20	NA
	2	12%	−0.26	−1.37	0.19	0.93
	3	12%	0.27	−0.67	0.13	0.69
18	0	42%	−1.11	NA	NA	NA
	1	36%	−0.60	−3.27	0.28	NA
	2	17%	−0.14	−1.48	0.22	1.78
	3	5%	0.43	0.39	0.14	1.87
19	0	53%	−1.01	NA	NA	NA
	1	20%	−0.54	−2.60	0.22	NA
	2	18%	−0.15	−1.12	0.17	1.48
	3	9%	0.36	−0.14	0.12	0.98
20	0	45%	−1.10	NA	NA	NA
	1	32%	−0.56	−2.86	0.24	NA
	2	16%	−0.12	−1.39	0.19	1.48
	3	7%	0.40	0.25	0.12	1.64

5 NONPARAMETRIC MEASUREMENT MODELS FOR RATING SCALE ANALYSIS

In addition to the models discussed so far in this book, it is also possible to use a nonparametric approach to explore rating scale functioning. In a measurement context, *nonparametric models* are defined as models whose estimation procedures do not involve parametric trans-formations of ordinal item responses to interval-level measures, as is done for all of the models that have been described so far in this book. Instead, nonparametric item response theory (IRT) models maintain the original ordinal scale on which item responses were observed. In addition, the model requirements or assumptions associated with nonparametric IRT models are often relatively less strict compared to those associated with parametric IRT models.

Researchers use nonparametric IRT approaches for numerous reasons. First, these models are useful in contexts where the assumptions or requirements for parametric IRT models may not be plausible or necessary (Junker & Sijtsma, 2001; Meijer & Baneke, 2004; Molenaar, 2001; Santor & Ramsay, 1998). For example, in some contexts, information about item or person ordering may be sufficient for the decisions that researchers need to make from a measurement procedure. For example, researchers may administer an attitude survey for the purpose of understanding the *relative order* of items and persons on a construct, but they may not need interval-level estimates (such as theta estimates for persons) for further analyses. Second, these models perform well with relatively smaller sample sizes than are required for parametric IRT model estimation. Specifically, when researchers apply parametric IRT models, meaningful interpretation of the estimates (e.g., item locations, person locations, and rating scale category thresholds) requires sufficient samples at each level of the construct to ensure that the estimates can be interpreted for the entire sample. Third, many researchers use nonparametric IRT models as an exploratory approach to examine basic measurement properties before they apply a parametric IRT model. Capturing the motivation for nonparametric IRT, Molenaar (2001) noted: "there remains a gap ... between the organized world of a mathematical measurement model and the messy world of real people reacting to a real set of items" (p. 295). Nonparametric IRT techniques are a promising alternative to para-metric IRT models that can be used in many measurement contexts, including rating scale analysis.

Table 5.1 Overview of Rating Scale Category Functioning Indices Based on Nonparametric Measurement Models

Groups of Indices	Guiding Question	Polytomous Nonparametric Measurement Models	
		Monotone Homogeneity Model	Double Monotonicity Model
Rating scale category ordering	To what extent do higher rating scale categories indicate higher locations on the construct?	Categories are ordered by definition	Categories are ordered by definition
Rating scale category precision	To what extent do individual rating scale categories reflect distinct ranges on the construct?	Precision indices specific to individual items	Precision indices specific to individual items

Table 5.1 applies indicators of rating scale category ordering and rating scale category precision to the selected nonparametric measurement models that are discussed in this chapter. The general motivation and use of these indicators are similar to the parametric models presented in Chapter 2 through Chapter 4. However, there are some differences specific to the nonparametric context. The CES-D scale data are used to demonstrate the interpretation and use of nonparametric indicators of rating scale functioning. Annotated statistical software syntax for each indicator is provided in the online supplement at **https:// study.sagepub.com/researchmethods/qass/wind-exploring-rating-scale-functioning**.

Mokken Scale Analysis

There are several approaches to nonparametric IRT in the literature that may be useful for rating scale analysis. In this volume, nonparametric analyses are conducted using models from Mokken Scale Analysis (MSA; Mokken, 1971). MSA is a theory-driven nonparametric approach to scaling items and persons in social science measurement procedures, such as attitude surveys and achievement tests. In contrast to atheoretical nonparametric methods, such as kernel smoothing (Ramsay, 1991) or kappa coefficients (Cohen, 1968), MSA uses a set of specific requirements about item response properties to evaluate measurement instruments from the perspective of invariance. In this sense, MSA shares a theoretical foundation with Rasch models, which are also based on invariance (see Chapter 2). Several authors have discussed theoretical and empirical similarities between Rasch measurement theory and MSA (Engelhard, 2008; Meijer et al., 1990; Wind, 2014).

In this section, we will consider foundational characteristics of MSA that are relevant to using this approach to conduct rating scale analysis. Readers who want to learn more about MSA may find the following introductory tutorials and instructional modules on MSA helpful:

Digital instructional module on Mokken scale analysis: https://ncme.elevate.commpartners.com/products/digital-module-03-nonparametric-item-response-theory

Sijtsma, K., & van der Ark, L. A. (2017). A tutorial on how to do a Mokken scale analysis on your test and questionnaire data. *British Journal of Mathematical and Statistical Psychology*, *70*(1), 137–158. https://doi.org/10.1111/bmsp.12078

Wind, S. A. (2017). An instructional module on Mokken scale analysis. *Educational Measurement: Issues and Practice*, *36*(2), 50–66. https://doi.org/10.1111/emip.12153

Overview of Mokken Models for Rating Scale Data

In its original presentation (Mokken, 1971), MSA included a procedure for analyzing dichotomous item responses using two nonparametric models: (1) the monotone homogeneity model (MHM), and (2) the double monotonicity model (DMM). Molenaar (1982, 1997) extended these techniques and models for use with polytomous responses, such as those obtained from survey instruments (Molenaar, 1982, 1997). These models provide researchers with a variety of numeric and graphical indicators of psychometric quality that can be used to inform practical decisions during scale revision and interpretation, including indicators of rating scale functioning (Wind, 2014).

Polytomous Monotone Homogeneity Model

The first model included in MSA is the MHM. In this chapter, we will focus on the polytomous formulation of the MHM, as presented by

128

Molenaar (1982, 1997). The MHM is based on three requirements. The first two requirements were discussed in Chapter 1: (1) *Unidimensionality*: One latent variable is necessary to explain most of the variation in item responses, (2) *Local independence*: After controlling for the primary latent variable, there is no statistical relationship between item responses. The third requirement is (3) *Monotonicity*: As participant locations on the latent variable increase, ordinal item responses are nondecreasing. Because MSA is nonparametric, it is necessary to use an indicator of person locations on the latent variable that does not require a parametric transformation. In practice, analysts who use MSA typically calculate *restscores* as indicators of participant locations on the latent variable that provide information about item quality, including rating scale functioning. Restscores are adjusted versions of total scores that do not include participant scores on an item of interest. Whereas total scores include responses to all of the items in the scale, restscores allow analysts to compare responses to an item of interest and the *rest* of the items. As a result, restscores provide information about item quality that is not biased by information from the item itself.

In the MHM, restscores are calculated as follows. First, participant total scores (X_+) are calculated as the sum of their responses to all of the items in the analysis. For example, in the CES-D scale, total scores are calculated for each participant as the sum of their responses to all 20 items. Then, separate restscores are calculated for each item by subtracting participant scores on the item of interest from their total score. For example, restscores specific to Item i are calculated as follows:

$$R_i = X_+ - X_i \tag{5.1}$$

In Equation 5.1, R_i is the restscore for Item i, X_+ is a participant's total score on all of the items in the analysis, and X_i is the participant's score on Item i. Restscores are item-specific because this allows analysts to evaluate the MHM requirements for each item without double-counting the item of interest. This technique is similar to using corrected item-total correlations to evaluate internal consistency for a scale in general survey research. In the case of the CES-D scale, each participant would have 20 item-specific restscores that correspond to each of the items in the scale.

When researchers evaluate the MHM requirements, they often combine participants into groups of people who have equal or adjacent restscores. These *restscore groups* improve statistical power for evaluating item characteristics because, in most applications, it is unlikely that there will be an equal number of participants who have each possible restscore. For details about the procedures used to construct restscore groups, please see Molenaar and Sijtsma (2000).

Evaluating Monotonicity

A first step in using the MHM is to evaluate the monotonicity requirement for each item in the scale. For polytomous Item i with categories that range from 0 to m ($k = 0, \ldots, m$), the monotonicity requirement is as follows. For participant groups A and B whose restscores (R) are ordered such that the average restscore for group A is lower than that of group B ($R_A < R_B$), the probability for a rating in or above a given category $P(x \geq k)$ should be lower for group A than that of group B. We can state this order requirement in equation format as:

$$P(x \geq k | R_A) \leq P(x \geq k | R_B), \tag{5.2}$$

for all $m - 1$ categories.

Figure 5.1 illustrates item monotonicity using Item 11 from the CES-D scale. The plots in this figure offer two related views of monotonicity for this item. First, Figure 5.1A illustrates monotonicity specific to individual categories in the rating scale. The x-axis shows item-specific restscore groups for Item 11, which range from 0 to 50. These groups are based on the distribution of restscores specific to Item 11 in the CES-D dataset. The y-axis shows a probability scale, which ranges from 0 to 1. Individual lines show the probability associated with categories in the rating scale. In MSA research, these lines are called Item Step Response Functions (ISRFs), and they are interpreted like the category-specific lines in the category probability plots for the GRM (see Figure 4.3). These lines show the probability for a rating in or above a certain category in the rating scale.

For example, the highest line in Figure 5.1A (solid line) shows the probability that participants in each restscore group will provide a rating in or above category 1. The middle line (dashed line) shows the probability that participants in each restscore group will provide a rating in or above category 2. Finally, the lowest line (dotted line) shows the probability that participants in each restscore group will provide a rating in or above category 3. Shading around each line shows a 95% confidence interval for the conditional probabilities. For the most part, these lines suggest that there is evidence of monotonicity for Item 11 because the lines have a generally positive (nondecreasing)

Figure 5.1 Example of Item Monotonicity Plots

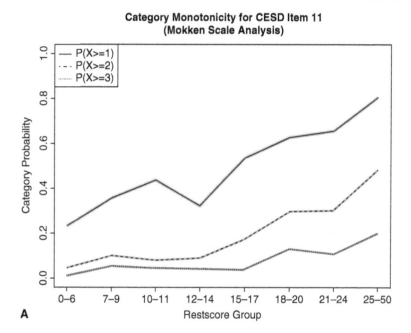

A

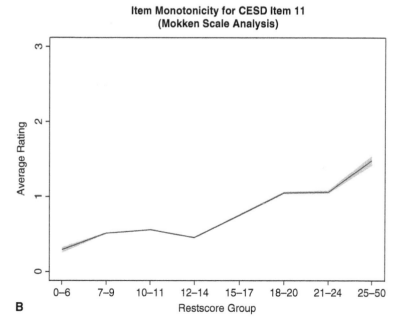

B

slope as the x-axis progresses from low restscores to high restscores. However, there was a notable violation of the monotonicity requirement for category 1 for participants with restscores that ranged from 10 to 14. We will consider this result later in the chapter.

It is also possible to evaluate monotonicity for an overall item, without specific attention to individual categories. This type of analysis provides an overall summary of item monotonicity that is sometimes simpler to interpret, use, and communicate than category-specific monotonicity results. Figure 5.1B illustrates this approach using a nonparametric item response function (IRF). The x-axis shows item-specific restscore groups for Item 11, which are the same as in Figure 5.1A. The y-axis shows the rating scale, which ranges from 0 to 3 for the CES-D scale. The line is the nonparametric IRF that shows the average ratings that were observed for Item 11 among participants in each restscore group. Shading around the line shows a 95% confidence interval for the conditional probabilities. This plot suggests that Item 11 generally adhered to the monotonicity requirement because the average ratings were generally nondecreasing as restscores increased. The slight negative slope between restscore groups 10–11 and 12–14 reflects the category-level probabilities illustrated in Figure 5.1A. We will consider this result later in this chapter.

In addition to graphical displays, it is also possible to evaluate monotonicity using statistical hypothesis tests, where a one-sided, one-sample Z-test is used to evaluate the null hypothesis that the cumulative probability for a rating in category k or higher is equal across adjacent restscore groups. Results from these comparisons can then be evaluated for statistical significance. For Item 11, there was one violation of monotonicity, as reflected in the plots in Figure 5.1.

Table 5.2 shows a numeric summary of results from the monotonicity analyses for the CES-D scale items. For each item, the magnitude of the largest monotonicity violation on the CES-D rating scale is presented. For example, for Item 11, the largest violation of monotonicity was a difference in average ratings of 0.11 points between participants in restscore groups 10–11 and 12–14, as we saw in Figure 5.1. Violations of monotonicity were present for all of the CES-D items except Item 2, Item 4, and Item 13. However, these violations were relatively minor for most items, with a maximum violation of 0.15 raw score points. In addition, for all but two items (Item 15 and Item 12), none of the violations of monotonicity were statistically significant. Item 15 had two statistically significant violations of monotonicity, and Item 12 had one statistically significant violation of monotonicity. Overall, these

Table 5.2 Overall MSA Results for the CES-D Scale

Item Number	Monotone Homogeneity Model				Double Monotonicity Model	
	Maximum Monotonicity Violation	Count of Statistically Significant Monotonicity Violations	Item Scalability		Maximum Invariant Item Ordering Violation	Count of Statistically Significant Invariant Item Ordering Violations
			H_i	SE		
1	0.08	0	0.20	0.02	0.33	3
2	0.00	0	0.24	0.02	0.24	2
3	0.07	0	0.26	0.02	0.25	4
4	0.00	0	0.20	0.02	0.29	5
5	0.07	0	0.26	0.02	0.21	1
6	0.07	0	0.24	0.02	0.25	6
7	0.04	0	0.25	0.02	0.38	7
8	0.06	0	0.19	0.02	0.27	2
9	0.07	0	0.22	0.02	0.20	2
10	0.08	0	0.24	0.02	0.22	0
11	0.11	0	0.22	0.02	0.25	3
12	0.15	1	0.13	0.02	0.32	1
13	0.00	0	0.22	0.02	0.34	4
14	0.05	0	0.25	0.02	0.25	3
15	0.14	2	0.19	0.02	0.34	8
16	0.10	0	0.14	0.02	0.38	3
17	0.04	0	0.23	0.02	0.12	0
18	0.09	0	0.23	0.02	0.29	2
19	0.04	0	0.23	0.02	0.23	1
20	0.11	0	0.23	0.02	0.21	1

results suggest that the CES-D items generally met the MHM requirement for monotonicity. Practically speaking, these results suggest that researchers can use MSA to explore the characteristics of the CES-D items, including rating scale functioning.

Evaluating Scalability

Analysts also evaluate adherence to the MHM using indicators of *scalability*. In the context of MSA, scalability is an indicator of the degree to which Guttman-type errors are associated with item responses. *Guttman errors* are easiest to understand when they are considered for dichotomous responses ($x = 0, 1$), but their principles also apply to rating scales. For dichotomous items, Guttman errors occur when a participant provides a correct or positive response to a relatively difficult item in combination with an incorrect or negative response to a relatively easier item. For rating scale (polytomous) items, Guttman errors occur when a participant responds in a higher category on a relatively difficult item *and also* responds in a lower category on a relatively easier item. For example, in the CES-D scale, we can imagine a Guttman error occurring between Item 1 (*I was bothered by things that usually don't bother me*) and Item 17 (*I had crying spells*). We saw in Chapter 2 that these items were ordered such that Item 1 was "easier" than Item 17, such that participants were more likely to respond in higher categories on Item 1 than Item 17. Given the order of these items, we would expect that participants who respond in high categories, such as *Most or All of the Time*, for Item 17 would also respond in a high category for Item 1. A Guttman error would occur if a participant responded *Most or All of the Time* to Item 17 and they also responded in a lower category, such as Category 1 (*Rarely or None of the Time*), to Item 1.

The practical implication of Guttman errors is that the difficulty order for items does not hold for some participants. As a result, total scores do not have the same interpretation for all participants. In MSA, scalability coefficients are indicators of the frequency and magnitude of Guttman errors associated with a set of items (H coefficients), item pairs (H_{ij} coefficients), and individual items (H_i coefficients). In the context of rating scale analysis, item-level scalability coefficients are most practically useful because they highlight Guttman errors in item responses specific to individual items, which may reflect idiosyncrasies related to rating scale categories. These coefficients are calculated as one minus the ratio of the frequency of observed Guttman errors for all item pairs associated with an item of interest to the frequency of Guttman errors that would be expected based on chance:

$$H_i = 1 - \frac{\sum_{i \neq j} F_{ij}}{\sum_{i \neq j} E_{ij}} \tag{5.3}$$

In Equation 5.3, F_{ij} is the observed frequency of Guttman errors, and E_{ij} is the expected frequency of Guttman errors. For polytomous items, Guttman errors are weighted based on the total number of errors involved in the response pattern associated with a particular pair of items (for details, see Molenaar, 1991 and Molenaar & Sijtsma, 2000, pp. 20–21).

Values of H_i that are positive indicate fewer Guttman errors than would be expected by chance for a given item. Values that are closer to 1.00 indicate fewer Guttman errors and support the use of an item to make inferences about participant ordering on the latent variable. Many researchers have adopted Mokken's (1971) criteria for evaluating item scalability: $H_i < 0.30$: unacceptable; $0.30 \leq H_i \leq 0.40$: weak scalability; $0.40 \leq H_i \leq 0.50$: medium scalability; $H_i \geq 0.50$: strong scalability. However, these values are simply suggestions based on previous research, and their usefulness varies across measurement contexts and their unique purposes and consequences.

For the CES-D, the scalability coefficient for the entire set of items was relatively low: $H = 0.22$ (SE = 0.01), suggesting that Guttman errors were prevalent among CES-D responses. Table 5.2 shows item-level scalability coefficients (H_i) for each of the individual items, along with standard errors (SE). All of the item-level scalability coefficients were positive—suggesting fewer Guttman errors than expected by chance alone. Item-level scalability coefficients ranged from $H_i = 0.13$ (SE = 0.02) for Item 12, which had the most frequent and extreme Guttman errors, to $H_i = 0.26$ (SE = 0.02) for Item 5, which had the fewest and least-extreme Guttman errors.

Polytomous Double Monotonicity Model

The second MSA model is the DMM. In this chapter, we will focus on the polytomous formulation of the DMM, as presented by Molenaar (1982, 1997). The DMM is based on four requirements. The first three are the same as the MHM: (1) *Unidimensionality*, (2) *Local independence*, and (3) *Monotonicity*. The fourth requirement is: (4) *Invariant item ordering* (IIO). IIO means that the relative item difficulty order is the same for all participants, regardless of their location on the latent variable. For example, in the CES-D scale, IIO would imply that the items could be ordered from low to high in terms of severity of depression required to exhibit a behavior, and this order would be the same for all participants. IIO is important in many measurement contexts because it ensures that there is a common item hierarchy that holds for all participants—thus facilitating clear interpretations of the scale (Meijer & Egberink, 2012).

Analysts who use MSA typically evaluate IIO at the overall item level, rather than within rating scale categories (Ligtvoet et al., 2010). For an overall item, the IIO assumption states that, if two items can be ordered such that Item i is more difficult than Item j for a fixed location on the latent variable (θ), then the probability of a correct or positive response on Item i is less than or equal to than that associated with Item j across the range of the latent variable (θ):

$$P_i(x|\theta) \le P_j(x|\theta). \tag{5.4}$$

In nonparametric IRT analyses, restscores (R) are used in place of theta estimates (θ), and IIO implies that:

$$P_i(x|R) \le P_j(x|R), \tag{5.5}$$

where $P_i(X|R)$ and $P_j(X|R)$ represent the probability succeeding on Item i and Item j, respectively across all values r of restscore R.

Evaluating Invariant Item Ordering

Figure 5.2 demonstrates a test for IIO at the overall item level using CES-D scale Item 1 and Item 17. The x-axis shows participant restscore groups specific to the item pair made up of Item 1 and Item 17. The y-axis shows the CES-D rating scale categories. Nonparametric IRFs are plotted for each item that show the average rating within each restscore group. The IRF for Item 1 is shown with a solid line, and the IRF Item 17 is shown with a dashed line. These items adhere to IIO because Item 1 always has lower average ratings compared to Item 17. As with monotonicity analyses, researchers can evaluate IIO using graphical displays such as Figure 5.2 as well as statistical hypothesis tests.

Table 5.2 shows results from the DMM analysis of the CES-D scale data. This analysis revealed violations of IIO for all of the CES-D items. The magnitude of these violations ranged from 0.12 to 0.38 raw

Figure 5.2 Illustration of Invariant Item Ordering

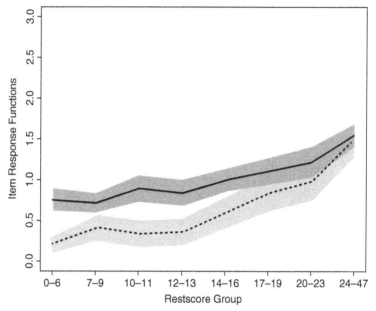

score scale points. All but two items (Item 10 and Item 17) had at least one statistically significant violation of IIO. Item 15 had the most frequent statistically significant violations of IIO (count = 8). Together, the results from the MHM and DMM suggest that the CES-D responses included some violations of important measurement properties that warrant further investigation. Rating scale analysis may provide insight into these idiosyncrasies.

Illustration of Rating Scale Analysis With Mokken Scale Analysis. In this section, the example CES-D scale data (see Chapter 1) are used to illustrate rating scale analysis with MSA. Table 5.3 provides a summary of numeric results from the MSA rating scale analysis for selected items; Table A.5.1 in the Appendix for this chapter includes results for all items. Likewise, when indices involve graphical displays, results are shown for selected items for the sake of brevity. In practice, one would examine all of the indices for all of the items in an analysis.

Table 5.3 Rating Scale Category Results From MSA (Selected Items)

Item	Rating Scale Category	% of Ratings	Average Participant Restscore Within Category	Count of Monotonicity Violations ≥0.03 Within Category	Maximum Monotonicity Violation Within Category
1	0	30%	13.41	NA	NA
	1	40%	15.31	0	0.02
	2	26%	19.84	1	0.08
	3	4%	27.67	1	0.03
3	0	60%	13.71	NA	NA
	1	17%	18.04	1	0.06
	2	13%	20.45	2	0.07
	3	10%	27.68	0	0.02
11	0	49%	13.25	NA	NA
	1	30%	17.40	1	0.11
	2	13%	23.33	0	0.02
	3	9%	23.26	0	0.02
12	0	32%	13.91	NA	NA
	1	29%	15.74	3	0.12
	2	28%	17.95	1	0.15
	3	11%	20.42	0	0.02
13	0	44%	13.41	NA	NA
	1	27%	15.71	0	0.01
	2	24%	21.71	0	0.00
	3	5%	25.16	0	0.01
15	0	45%	13.70	NA	NA
	1	29%	16.42	1	0.11
	2	19%	20.97	1	0.14
	3	6%	24.63	1	0.03

Note: The Appendix includes results for all CES-D scale items.

All of the analyses were conducted using the "mokken" package for R (van der Ark, 2007, 2012). Annotated code for conducting these analyses is provided in the online supplement at **https://study.sagepub.com/research methods/qass/wind-exploring-rating-scale-functioning**.

138

Rating Scale Category Ordering

Like the Graded Response Model (see Chapter 4), polytomous MSA models are defined using cumulative category probabilities. This means that rating scale categories are always ordered by definition within items. As a result, it is not possible to directly evaluate category ordering using polytomous MSA models.[1]

However, monotonicity indicators for rating scale categories based on the polytomous MHM still provide insight into to the overall orientation of rating scale categories. Accordingly, we will examine three indicators of rating scale ordering in this section: Average restscores within rating scale categories, graphical displays of rating scale category monotonicity, and numeric indicators of rating scale category monotonicity.

Average Participant Restscores Within Rating Scale Categories for Individual Items

As one indicator of rating scale category ordering, analysts can examine average participant restscores within rating scale categories for each item. This analysis provides an overall indicator of the direction of a rating scale. For example, in the CES-D scale, we expect that participants who responded in higher categories had equal or higher restscores than participants who responded in lower categories. Such correspondence between restscores and scale categories would suggest that higher categories in the CES-D scale reflected higher levels of depression.

Table 5.3 includes average participant restscores within rating scale categories for selected CES-D items. These results indicate that participant restscores followed the expected order: As categories progressed from low to high, so did the average restscores for all of the CES-D items. This result provides support for interpreting higher rating scale categories as indicators of higher levels of depression for all items in the CES-D.

---

[1]Wind (2016) proposed an approach related to MSA in which the MHM can be reformulated to use adjacent-categories probabilities as a method for examining category ordering. This method has not been widely adopted, but preliminary results suggest that it is a promising approach to identifying deviations from expected category ordering for polytomous item responses.

Counts of Item-Specific Violations of Category Monotonicity

It is also possible to use monotonicity analyses from the MHM to explore rating scale category ordering. Recall from Figure 5.1A that we can explore monotonicity for survey items specific to rating scale categories and from Figure 5.1B that we can explore monotonicity for an overall item. When items exhibit monotonicity, this provides support for interpreting the rating scale in the intended order.

As we saw earlier, we can evaluate monotonicity numerically by calculating the magnitude of monotonicity violations on the raw score scale. In some cases, it may be useful to evaluate these violations using tests for statistical significance. However, when the focus of monotonicity analyses is on rating scale categories, such significance tests may not be necessary or appropriate. In addition, significance tests for category-level monotonicity are not common in applied MSA research. Instead, researchers may find it more useful to examine the frequency and magnitude of violations of monotonicity for categories, without tests for statistical significance. More frequent and larger violations of monotonicity indicate that the interpretation of the rating scale categories may not hold across participants with different restscores.

To illustrate, Table 5.3 provides the frequency of monotonicity violations that exceeded 0.03 for each cumulative category probability ($P(x \geq 1)$; $P(x \geq 2)$; $P(x \geq 3)$) specific to individual items in the CES-D scale. The value 0.03 was selected because it is the typical minimum value used to identify violations of monotonicity in MSA (van der Ark, 2012). Table 5.3 also provides the maximum value of violations of monotonicity specific to each cumulative category probability. For the CES-D scale data, the frequency of violations ranged from 0 to 3, and the magnitude of violations ranged from 0 to 0.15 raw score scale points. The most frequent violations of monotonicity (count = 3) and the largest violation of monotonicity (0.15 raw score points) both occurred for Item 12. There were also several items for which no violations of monotonicity were observed, such as Item 13. These results suggest that additional investigation may be warranted to more fully understand participants' interpretation and use of the CES-D rating scale categories.

Graphical Displays of Cumulative Category Monotonicity for Individual Items

It is also possible to explore category ordering using graphical displays of category monotonicity, such as Figure 5.1A. When rating scale categories adhere to monotonicity, these plots show nondecreasing category probabilities over increasing restscores. Recall from Figure 5.1A that Item 11 in the CES-D scale generally adhered to monotonicity within rating scale categories because the cumulative probabilities had a generally positive slope. However, there were some violations of monotonicity. Such violations of monotonicity within rating scale categories indicate that the interpretation of the rating scale categories may not hold across participants with different restscores. For Item 11, there was a clear violation of monotonicity between the third restscore group ($10 \leq R_{11} \leq 11$) and the fourth restscore group ($12 \leq R_{11} \leq 14$). Specifically, the probability for a rating in category 1 or higher ($P(x \geq 1)$; solid line) decreased between these two restscore groups. This decrease corresponded to a lower average rating on Item 11 among participants in the fourth restscore group compared to those in the third restscore group. This violation of monotonicity suggests that participants' interpretation of the CES-D rating scale categories for Item 11 may not be consistent with their interpretation of the rating scale categories for other CES-D items, at least among participants in the fourth restscore group.

Figure 5.3 shows examples of monotonicity plots for Items 1, 15, 3, and 11 in the CES-D scale. All four of these items generally adhered to monotonicity, but there were some violations specific to certain ranges of the total score. Together, these results suggest that, for several items, certain groups of participants may have interpreted the order or orientation of the rating scale differently from other participants. However, the overall magnitude of monotonicity violations was relatively small for items in the CES-D scale. Researchers who are interested in ensuring a consistent interpretation of category ordering for all participants could consider item-specific violations in detail for the participants with restscore groups associated with monotonicity violations.

Rating Scale Category Precision

It is also possible to use nonparametric IRT methods from MSA to evaluate the precision of rating scale categories. We will examine two indicators of rating scale category precision in this section: distinct cumulative category probabilities and discriminating cumulative category probabilities.

Distinct Cumulative Category Probabilities for Individual Items

In addition to their usefulness for examining category ordering, graphical displays of cumulative category probabilities based on the

Figure 5.3 Cumulative Category Probability Plots for Selected CES-D Items Based on MSA

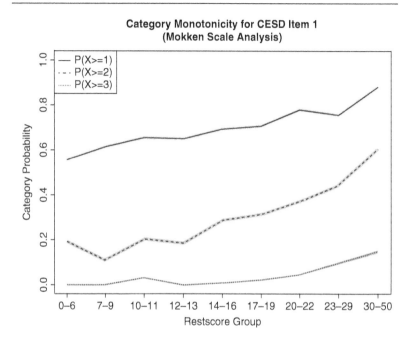

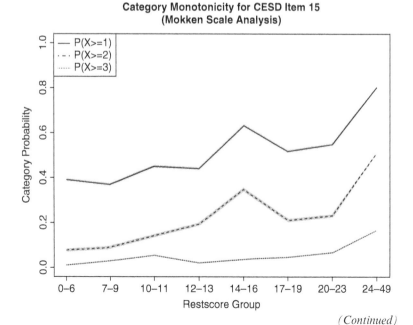

(Continued)

Figure 5.3 Cumulative Category Probability Plots for Selected CES-D Items Based on MSA *(Continued)*

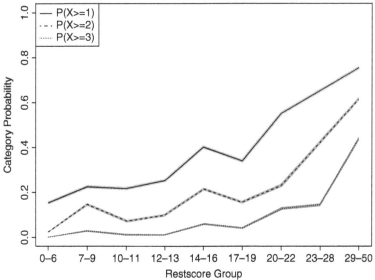

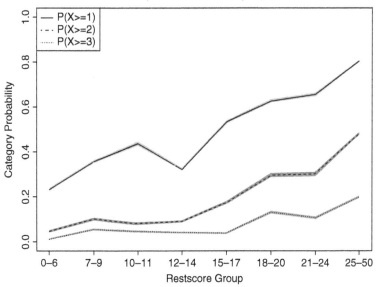

MHM can provide insight into the degree to which the categories in a rating scale provide unique information about participants with regard to the construct. Researchers can examine cumulative category probability plots for evidence that each category describes unique levels of the latent variable. In the nonparametric MSA context, this means that participants who have different restscores have different probabilities for responding in each category. Ideally, participants with lower restscores would be substantially less likely to respond in higher categories compared to participants with higher restscores.

To evaluate this property, researchers can examine the distance between cumulative category probabilities (e.g., Figure 5.1A) specific to individual items. Very small distances between the cumulative probabilities would indicate that there is not much distinction between rating scale categories—that is, participants who select one category may not have meaningfully distinct locations on the latent variable from participants who select the next-highest category. In this case, researchers may consider using fewer categories in the rating scale or revising category descriptions to better reflect differences among participants. Conversely, very large distances between the cumulative probabilities would indicate that rating scale categories may not effectively distinguish between participants. In this case, additional categories may be needed to better understand differences among participants. Categories demonstrate precision when the distance between cumulative category probabilities is large enough to identify participants with meaningful differences on the latent variable and small enough to provide appropriate distinction among participants.

The cumulative category plots in Figure 5.3 show different patterns of category distinctiveness. For example, the plot for Item 3 shows moderate distances between category probabilities, and the distance between the cumulative category probabilities is relatively evenly spaced across the range of participant restscores. For Item 11, there was a larger difference between the probabilities for the lower categories $P(x \geq 1)$ and $P(x \geq 2)$ compared to the difference between the probabilities for the higher categories ($P(x \geq 2)$ and $P(x \geq 3)$)—suggesting some differences in category distinctiveness for this item.

Item 1 is an example of an item with notably large distances between category probabilities that persist across the range of restscores. For this item, there is a substantial difference in the probability for a rating in category 1 or higher compared to the probability for a rating in category 2 or higher, and in category 3 or higher. Although somewhat

144

less extreme, this pattern is also true for Item 15, particularly between $P(x \geq 1)$ and $P(x \geq 2)$. These results suggest that the middle categories $P(x \geq 2)$ of the CES-D rating scale may not provide distinct information from the higher categories $P(x \geq 3)$.

Discriminating Item-Specific Cumulative Category Probabilities

In addition to considering the distance between cumulative category probabilities, researchers can also examine graphical displays of cumulative category probabilities for evidence of appropriate levels of discrimination specific to each item. In the nonparametric MSA context, slope parameters are not estimated for these category probabilities, as is the case in parametric IRT models such as the Generalized Partial Credit Model (see Chapter 4). In addition, as long as they adhere to monotonicity, MSA permits categories to exhibit different slopes within items. This property allows researchers to evaluate category probabilities for differences in discrimination.

The role of category discrimination varies across assessment contexts. In some cases, it may be important for cumulative category probabilities to exhibit steep slopes, such that they sharply identify differences among participants. In other cases, such sharp distinctions may be less important. Researchers can use nonparametric IRT methods based on MSA to detect differences in category discrimination across items that may be important for the interpretation, use, and revision of rating scales.

Returning to Figure 5.3, we can now consider differences in cumulative category probabilities across CES-D scale items. For Item 3, all three cumulative category probabilities had moderate discrimination that generally persisted across the range of restscores. In contrast, the cumulative category probability slopes for Item 1 were relatively flat for most restscore groups. This result suggests that for Item 1, the CES-D rating scale categories did not distinguish among participants with different levels of depression. Similarly, the cumulative category probabilities for Item 15 and Item 11 were relatively flat across most of the lower restscore groups ($R_{15} \leq 13$), but had a moderate slope for participants with higher restscores. These items are examples of differences in discrimination across categories within an item. In the context of the CES-D, this finding may suggest that Item 15 and Item 11 are effective for distinguishing among participants who have moderate-to-high levels of depression, but that they are not effective for identifying less-extreme differences in depression levels.

Chapter Summary

In this chapter, we explored how researchers can use nonparametric measurement models from Mokken Scale Analysis (MSA) to examine the overall psychometric quality of their scales, and to evaluate rating scale functioning for individual items. We used two models from MSA: (1) the Monotone Homogeneity Model (MHM), and (2) the Double Monotonicity Model (DMM). These two models allowed us to evaluate the CES-D scale items for evidence of useful psychometric properties, including rating scale ordering and rating scale category precision, using nonparametric techniques. The nonparametric approach allowed us to consider item functioning overall and rating scale functioning within items with less-strict assumptions and requirements than the parametric models, such as those in Chapters 3 and 4.

In an overall analysis of the CES-D scale items with MSA models, we learned that many of the items had violations of monotonicity, some susceptibility to Guttman errors, and some violations of invariant item ordering. However, the magnitude of each of these problematic characteristics was relatively small for individual items in the scale. This result suggests that the CES-D scale functioned relatively well as a whole, but that additional investigation was warranted to identify and understand idiosyncrasies for individual items. We used rating scale analysis techniques to explore the items further.

First, we used MSA to examine the orientation (i.e., direction) of the CES-D rating scale. We used graphical displays and numeric indicators of monotonicity to evaluate whether participants interpreted and used the rating scale categories in the intended order. For the CES-D scale, we saw that the rating scale categories were generally oriented correctly. However, there were some discrepancies in how some groups of participants with different levels of depression interpreted and used the categories for some of the items.

Next, we used MSA to evaluate the degree to which the categories in the CES-D rating scale provided distinct information. We examined plots of cumulative category probabilities specific to each item to explore how the rating scale categories distinguished among participants with different levels of depression. Specifically, we examined the space between cumulative category probabilities and the slope of these probabilities across participant restscore groups. We saw that the CES-D rating scale generally distinguished between participants with different levels of depression, but there were some differences in distinctiveness across items. We also saw that there were some differences in how the scale categories distinguished among participants *within* items. For example, some items were more effective at distinguishing between moderate and high depression levels than they were for participants with lower levels of depression.

Overall, the nonparametric techniques in this chapter provided an exploratory approach to evaluating the psychometric properties of survey items, including rating scale functioning. Compared to the parametric models presented in earlier chapters, the nonparametric approach provided a more detailed look at not only *whether* there were some potential issues related to rating scale functioning, but *how* and *for which participants* these issues occurred. For this reason, nonparametric techniques such as MSA may be a useful initial analysis to help researchers explore and understand their data before they select a parametric model.

APPENDIX

Table A.5.1 Rating Scale Category Results From MSA: All CES-D Scale Items

Item	Rating Scale Category	% of Ratings	Average Participant Restscore Within Category	Count of Monotonicity Violations ≥0.03 Within Category	Maximum Monotonicity Violation Within Category
1	0	30%	13.41	NA	NA
	1	40%	15.31	0	0.02
	2	26%	19.84	1	0.08
	3	4%	27.67	1	0.03
2	0	50%	13.10	NA	NA
	1	25%	16.96	0	0.00
	2	17%	22.59	0	0.02
	3	8%	24.69	0	0.01
3	0	60%	13.71	NA	NA
	1	17%	18.04	1	0.06
	2	13%	20.45	2	0.07
	3	10%	27.68	0	0.02
4	0	51%	13.62	NA	NA
	1	22%	16.95	0	0.02
	2	18%	20.64	0	0.00
	3	10%	23.42	0	0.02
5	0	40%	12.23	NA	NA
	1	32%	16.44	1	0.07
	2	24%	21.45	0	0.02
	3	4%	29.49	0	0.02
6	0	51%	13.26	NA	NA
	1	25%	17.00	2	0.06
	2	16%	22.18	2	0.07
	3	7%	26.69	0	0.02

(Continued)

Table A.5.1 Rating Scale Category Results From MSA: All CES-D Scale Items *(Continued)*

Item	Rating Scale Category	% of Ratings	Average Participant Restscore Within Category	Count of Monotonicity Violations ≥0.03 Within Category	Maximum Monotonicity Violation Within Category
7	0	47%	12.99	NA	NA
	1	27%	16.83	0	0.00
	2	17%	20.73	0	0.02
	3	9%	27.22	1	0.04
8	0	44%	13.39	NA	NA
	1	21%	16.63	2	0.06
	2	21%	18.51	2	0.06
	3	13%	22.87	0	0.02
9	0	56%	13.87	NA	NA
	1	22%	17.85	1	0.05
	2	13%	20.63	1	0.07
	3	9%	25.49	0	0.02
10	0	53%	13.38	NA	NA
	1	22%	16.81	1	0.08
	2	19%	21.94	1	0.07
	3	7%	26.23	0	0.02
11	0	49%	13.25	NA	NA
	1	30%	17.40	1	0.11
	2	13%	23.33	0	0.02
	3	9%	23.26	0	0.02
12	0	32%	13.91	NA	NA
	1	29%	15.74	3	0.12
	2	28%	17.95	1	0.15
	3	11%	20.42	0	0.02
13	0	44%	13.41	NA	NA
	1	27%	15.71	0	0.01
	2	24%	21.71	0	0.00
	3	5%	25.16	0	0.01

(Continued)

Table A.5.1 Rating Scale Category Results From MSA: All CES-D Scale Items *(Continued)*

Item	Rating Scale Category	% of Ratings	Average Participant Restscore Within Category	Count of Monotonicity Violations ≥0.03 Within Category	Maximum Monotonicity Violation Within Category
14	0	55%	13.25	NA	NA
	1	20%	17.65	0	0.01
	2	17%	22.15	2	0.05
	3	8%	26.34	0	0.02
15	0	45%	13.70	NA	NA
	1	29%	16.42	1	0.11
	2	19%	20.97	1	0.14
	3	6%	24.63	1	0.03
16	0	37%	14.16	NA	NA
	1	27%	15.22	1	0.06
	2	25%	19.15	1	0.10
	3	10%	20.57	1	0.06
17	0	64%	14.20	NA	NA
	1	12%	18.24	1	0.04
	2	12%	21.30	0	0.03
	3	12%	24.68	1	0.03
18	0	42%	12.73	NA	NA
	1	36%	17.33	1	0.09
	2	17%	21.56	1	0.04
	3	5%	26.68	1	0.04
19	0	53%	13.40	NA	NA
	1	20%	17.24	1	0.03
	2	18%	20.98	1	0.04
	3	9%	25.84	0	0.01
20	0	45%	13.09	NA	NA
	1	32%	17.09	1	0.04
	2	16%	21.05	2	0.11
	3	7%	26.78	1	0.05

6 SUMMARY AND RESOURCES FOR FURTHER STUDY

This chapter reviews the purpose of rating scale analysis and provides a summary of the major concepts from the previous chapters. In addition, this chapter revisits and elaborates on practical considerations related to rating scale analysis to help readers make informed decisions with their results. The chapter concludes with a discussion of resources for further study.

What Is Rating Scale Analysis?

Rating scale analysis is a set of techniques and procedures that researchers can use to ensure that the rating scales that accompany their survey items have a meaningful interpretation and use. Researchers often use rating scale analysis to gather evidence to help them improve their rating scales in future administrations or to inform decisions about how to interpret and use their survey data. Rating scale analysis provides information about the psychometric quality of item responses that is distinct from other psychometric indicators, such as internal consistency statistics (e.g., alpha), factor analysis, and many item response theory (IRT) analyses that focus on overall item difficulty estimates. Rating scale analysis focuses on ensuring that the interpretation and use of ordinal scale categories is meaningful for an entire set of items, within individual items, within sets of items, or within subgroups of participants. Evidence of acceptable rating scale functioning ensures meaningful interpretation of the directionality of rating scales, informs the interpretation of differences between categories, and ensures a comparable interpretation of categories between items, components of a scale, or subgroups of items or persons. Just as it is important to evaluate survey instruments for evidence of validity, reliability, and fairness in each sample and setting (American Educational Research Association (AERA) et al., 2014), it is also necessary to evaluate rating scale functioning with each application of a measurement instrument.

In this book, we explored methods for rating scale analysis that use measurement models based on Rasch measurement theory (see Chapters 2 and 3; Rasch, 1960), non-Rasch IRT models (see Chapter 4), and nonparametric measurement techniques from Mokken Scale Analysis (MSA; Mokken, 1971; see Chapter 5). Each of these approaches provides analysts with information about rating scale functioning that can inform the interpretation and use of survey instruments. Table 1.2 provided an overview of the major characteristics and considerations of these approaches for rating scale analysis.

Summary of Previous Chapters

This book began with a theoretical discussion of rating scale functioning from the perspective of IRT. Then, methods for evaluating rating scale functioning were discussed and illustrated using example data from the CES-D scale (Radloff, 1977). The first set of rating scale analysis methods was presented using three polytomous Rasch models (Rasch, 1960), which have several properties that make them particularly well suited for rating scale analysis. The selected Rasch models for rating scale analysis included the Rating Scale Model (RSM; Andrich, 1978), the Partial Credit Model (PCM; Masters, 1982), and the Partial Credit formulation of the Many-Facet Rasch Model (PC-MFRM; Linacre, 1989). Researchers who use a Rasch approach to rating scale analysis typically do so because it offers a theoretical framework to evaluate instruments against well-defined measurement properties, including invariant measurement. The Rasch approach to rating scale analysis allows researchers to evaluate their survey instruments for adherence to Rasch model requirements, while also providing practical information about rating scale functioning. Specifically, each of the Rasch models included in this book provides information about *rating scale category ordering* or the degree to which participants' empirical use of rating scale categories reflects the hypothesized order of the categories, given the ordinal rating scale. These models also provide information about *rating scale category precision* or the degree to which rating scale categories identify participants who have meaningfully different locations on the construct. The PC-MFRM allows researchers to compare rating scale category ordering and rating scale category precision across levels of explanatory facets, such as subgroups of participants or subsets of items. In our analyses of the CES-D scale data, we used the PC-MFRM to explore rating scale functioning specific to subgroups of participants who had different levels of education.

Next, rating scale analysis methods based on non-Rasch models were presented and illustrated using the Generalized Partial Credit Model (GPCM) (Muraki, 1997; Muraki & Muraki, 2018), which is a polytomous IRT model with an item discrimination parameter, and the Graded Response Model (GRM) (Samejima, 1997, 2018), which is a

152

polytomous IRT model based on cumulative probabilities. These models provide similar types of information about rating scale functioning as polytomous Rasch models, but researchers typically use them for different reasons. Specifically, researchers who are interested in *evaluating* item responses for evidence that they conform with fundamental measurement properties, such as invariance, often use a Rasch approach. On the other hand, researchers who are interested in *selecting a model* that best reflects the characteristics of their data may choose a non-Rasch polytomous IRT model such as the GPCM or GRM. All of the Rasch and non-Rasch IRT models covered in this book provide researchers with information about category ordering and precision. The major difference is that non-Rasch models do so while considering additional aspects of item responses, such as differences in item discrimination. Rasch models would generally identify such differences as violations of measurement requirements (see Table 1.2).

In Chapter 5, we saw how researchers can use nonparametric measurement models to explore rating scale functioning for survey instruments. Specifically, MSA (Mokken, 1971) was presented as a nonparametric approach to rating scale analysis. Researchers typically select MSA when they want to use a measurement framework to evaluate item responses for evidence of useful properties, but when it may not be necessary or appropriate to apply a parametric model. For example, researchers may opt for a nonparametric approach when they have small samples, when their analytic goals require only ordinal (rather than interval) descriptions of item and person ordering on a latent variable, or when they are exploring a construct that does not lend itself to an interval-level representation (Meijer & Baneke, 2004). Researchers may also use MSA when they want a detailed view of item characteristics, including rating scale characteristics, for participants with different locations on the latent variable. The graphical displays in MSA facilitate such explorations (DeCastellarnau, 2018).

Table A.6.1 in the Appendix at the end of this chapter provides a list of rating scale functioning indicators and relevant evidence that correspond to the models included in this book. Each model and each indicator provides unique information about rating scale functioning that should be interpreted with respect to the unique goals and context of each analysis. Depending on the context, some indicators may be more or less important than others. Rather than using the techniques presented in this book as a checklist, readers are encouraged to consider the role of rating scale functioning for a particular analysis and select and interpret relevant indicators relative to the measurement context.

How Should a Researcher Select a Model for Rating Scale Analysis?

As we saw in this book, researchers have numerous options for models that facilitate rating scale analysis, including Rasch models, non-Rasch IRT models, and nonparametric measurement models. All of these approaches provide useful information about rating scale analysis. So, how should a researcher select an approach? As we often say in the social sciences, "it depends." In the case of rating scale analysis, researchers should select a model that meets their overall modeling goals, reflects their practical goals, and that will provide information that is useful and accessible for their target audiences.

Overall Modeling Goals

Models that facilitate rating scale analysis correspond to different overall modeling goals. Researchers who are concerned with evaluating their survey data within a framework that clearly defines how measurement *should* work in the social sciences may benefit most from a Rasch measurement theory (Rasch, 1960) approach to rating scale analysis. As we noted in Chapter 2, Rasch models were developed for the purpose of helping researchers evaluate their item responses against measurement requirements derived from physical laws of measurement. As a result, these models are strict—they identify deviations from fundamental measurement properties, such as unidimensionality, local independence, and invariance, as areas where a measurement procedure deviates from an ideal structure. Researchers use these deviations as a means to learn more about their latent variable(s), learn more about their participants, and to make improvements to a measurement procedure. Because they require adherence to fundamental measurement properties, Rasch models offer practical benefits that are useful in applied survey research contexts. For example, when there is good fit to a Rasch model, researchers can describe item and person locations on a single linear continuum and illustrate these locations in a comprehensive and relatively simple visual display (i.e., a Wright map). Thus, the Rasch approach can be summarized as a strict but theoretically and practically beneficial approach for researchers who want to evaluate their instruments and provide a simple and accessible description of a latent variable that holds across items and persons.

On the other hand, researchers who are concerned with accurately representing the characteristics of their survey data in their model

154

estimates may not wish to use a Rasch approach. Instead, these researchers often select a model from several candidate IRT models that include parameters that reflect practical realities of survey data, such as differences in item slope (i.e., item discrimination). Rather than the *requirements* that characterize Rasch models, these non-Rasch IRT models make *assumptions* about item responses. For example, the GPCM and GRM (see Chapter 4) assume unidimensionality and local independence, but these assumptions are not tied to a theoretical framework. As a result, researchers may apply several models to their data and compare them using global model-fit comparison tests to identify a model that most accurately reflects their data. Some researchers find this approach useful when they are not especially interested in revising their instruments or refining their theory about a latent variable, but instead wish to obtain person and item parameter estimates that accurately reflect an administration of a survey instrument.

Finally, the MSA approach that we considered in Chapter 5 provides researchers with a theoretically based but mathematically conservative approach to modeling survey data. Researchers who use MSA models in their survey analyses do so because they want to evaluate their item responses for evidence of important measurement properties, but wish to maintain the original ordinal scale of measurement. Reasons for maintaining an ordinal scale of measurement could be theoretical: there may not be a sufficient theoretical foundation for a latent variable to justify representing it with an interval-level scale, practical: there may not be a need for interval-level person and item estimates, or exploratory: researchers may wish to start with an ordinal approach to first learn about their item response characteristics before deciding on a modeling approach. In addition, some researchers opt for a nonparametric approach when they are working with small samples or otherwise cannot justify applying a parametric model to their data (Meijer & Baneke, 2004).

Practical Goals for Rating Scale Analysis

Researchers' choice of a model should also be informed by their practical goals for rating scale analysis. There are some important differences in the types of information that the models presented in this book provide, and these differences can help researchers choose an approach to rating scale analysis.

First, researchers should consider whether they need information about rating scale functioning specific to each item. In some cases, it may be appropriate to obtain an overall picture of rating scale functioning that does not distinguish between individual items. For example, researchers who want to verify that, overall, their rating scale is functioning appropriately, may select the RSM, which does not include item-specific rating scale category information. In some cases, researchers begin with a model that offers item-specific details, but then switch to the RSM based on empirical evidence that there is not much difference in rating scale functioning between items. If researchers would like to evaluate rating scale functioning for individual items, then they will likely select among models with item-specific threshold parameters, such as the PCM, GPCM, and GRM. MSA also provides item-specific details about rating scale functioning but in a nonparametric context. Finally, if researchers wish to evaluate rating scale functioning specific to explanatory variables in a measurement procedure, such as participant subgroups or item subsets, the PC-MFRM offers such details. This model is particularly flexible, and researchers can use it to examine rating scale functioning across various aspects of their data.

Next, researchers should consider the importance of rating scale category ordering in their survey research context. In this book, we saw how researchers can use results from rating scale analysis to empirically gauge whether responses in higher rating scale categories (e.g., *Strongly Agree* or *Often*) reflect higher levels of a latent variable (e.g., higher levels of empathy or more severe depression) and vice versa. Although each of the models presented in this book provides some information about the directionality of scale categories, there are important differences in how the models deal with potential category disordering. Some measurement models are specified such that the threshold parameters empirically identify category disordering. Among the models included in this book, these *adjacent-categories* models include the RSM, PCM, PC-MFRM, and GPCM. Researchers who want to identify disordered categories to ensure that their scale is oriented in the correct direction may opt for one of these models. For example, category ordering analyses are particularly important in situations where researchers want to verify the correct placement of a category within a scale, such as a neutral category (discussed further later in this chapter). Conversely, if researchers want general information about scale orientation, but category ordering is not of primary concern, they may select a model such as the GRM, which estimates thresholds using *cumulative probabilities*. These models define the threshold parameters so that they are always in the expected order.

156

Considerations Related to Audience

Finally, it is important to keep in mind how results from rating scale analysis will be used and communicated. If a researcher is conducting rating scale analysis for a general audience (e.g., for a policy report or a presentation to practitioners), detailed item-level results about rating scale functioning may not be needed. In these cases, a relatively simple model that lends itself to a succinct set of results about scale order and precision may be appropriate; the RSM may be a useful choice in this case. Likewise, if an audience is not accustomed to interpreting results on a logit scale, a nonparametric approach such as MSA may be useful. However, if researchers wish to share detailed information to inform next steps in a psychometric study or procedure, more complex models may be appropriate.

Practical Takeaways: How Can a Researcher Use Results From Rating Scale Analysis?

After a rating scale analysis is conducted, researchers usually need to do something with their results. In this section, we consider some practical takeaways for next steps after rating scale analysis.

What Should I Do If My Scale Categories Are Disordered?

If a rating scale analysis reveals disordered categories, it is not appropriate to interpret ratings in the intended order. For example, in Chapter 3, the PCM revealed disordered categories for several items in the CES-D scale. When this happens, researchers have several options. An important first step is to consider potential reasons for the disordering using the item content, scale labels or descriptions, theory, and literature. If possible, it is particularly useful to conduct mixed-methods analyses using think-aloud or cognitive interviews (Padilla & Leighton, 2017) to understand how participants interpreted and used the scale categories to respond to the item(s), which may provide potential explanations for the disordered categories. If there is a content-related reason for disordering, a good next step is to revise the item, category label(s), or category descriptions, and readminister the survey in a pilot test to see if the revisions result in expected category order.

In addition to qualitative and theoretical considerations, numeric characteristics of item responses can sometimes contribute to category disordering. Specifically, a pair of rating scale category thresholds can be disordered if there are very few observations in the higher category. For example, we saw from the PCM in Chapter 3 and the GPCM in Chapter 4 that the second and third thresholds for CES-D scale Item 11 were disordered, *and* that there was a relatively low (<10%) frequency of responses in category 3 compared to category 2. This low frequency in category 3 may have contributed to the threshold disordering. In such situations, some researchers have suggested that analysts can consider combining (i.e., collapsing) adjacent rating scale categories into fewer categories that include more responses (Wetzel & Carstensen, 2014). Category collapsing may also be appropriate if the results from content analyses or cognitive interviews suggest that participants interpreted adjacent categories in a similar way. However, this potential solution should be approached cautiously for several reasons. First, collapsing categories changes the data from how the items were presented to participants. Accordingly, the collapsed version of the scale no longer reflects the instrument in its original form—thus potentially compromising the interpretation of the results as representative of the participants' actual use of the instrument. Second, there are many ways to combine categories, and each solution has different implications for modeling results. For example, a researcher may decide to combine category 2 and category 3 for Item 11 in the CES-D scale given the PCM and GPCM results. However, another researcher may decide to combine categories 1, 2, *and* 3 to create a dichotomous version of Item 11. If the analysis is conducted using a model with separate thresholds for each item such as the PCM, it would be possible to analyze the data with a dichotomous version of Item 11 and four-category scales for the remaining items. Especially when disordering occurs in central scale categories, there are numerous potential combinations that could result in reformulations of rating scales that would lead to different rating scale structures. In practice, a good strategy for collapsing categories is to explore the results from several potential solutions before deciding on a restructured version of a rating scale for some or all items.

If the reason for rating scale category disordering is not clearly tied to content or the distribution of responses across categories, researchers should proceed with caution in including the item(s) with disordered categories in analyses that require total scores. When scale categories are disordered, the interpretation of ratings for items with disordered

158

categories may not be comparable to that of items with the expected category ordering. If appropriate, given content validity considerations, analysts may consider omitting such items from these analyses.

What Should I Do If My Scale Categories Are Imprecise?

All of the models included in this book provide information to help researchers determine whether their rating scale categories are precise. When rating scale analysis reveals that categories are *imprecise*, this means that one or more categories in the scale does not provide unique information about participants in terms of the latent variable. For example, in Chapter 3, the PCM revealed that the middle categories ($x = 1$ and $x = 2$) of the CES-D rating scale did not provide unique information about participants' depression levels for Item 3 and Item 11 (among other items). This situation calls for similar considerations as category disordering. Specifically, if possible, analysts should attempt to understand why categories did not provide distinct information. Content analyses of item stems, scale category labels, or scale category descriptions may provide insight. In addition, researchers may consult theory or literature to identify potential content-related or theoretical reasons for nondistinct categories. Think-aloud and cognitive interviews may also help analysts understand how participants interpreted and used categories in ways that may have contributed to the lack of precision. Researchers can use results from these analyses to revise item or category content to potentially improve category precision in future administrations of the instrument. When it is not possible to revise and readminister the scale, analysts may cautiously consider combining or collapsing categories using an exploratory and thoughtful approach as discussed earlier for disordered categories.

It is also possible for rating scale categories to describe a range of the latent variable that is too large for a meaningful interpretation. In this case, additional categories may be needed to distinguish between participants who have meaningful differences in the latent variable. Content analyses, considerations of theory and literature, and qualitative techniques such as think-aloud or cognitive interviews may provide insight into additional levels that could be represented in a rating scale for some or all items. However, unlike the situation where categories describe too narrow a range of the latent variable, it is not possible to address this situation by recoding participant responses. Instead, researchers could consider pilot-testing a new version of the rating scale that includes additional categories to improve category precision in future administrations.

How Do I Know If My Neutral Category Is Meaningful?

Rating scale analyses are particularly useful when researchers want to use empirical evidence to determine whether the neutral category in their rating scale has a meaningful interpretation. As we discussed throughout this book, category ordering analyses can help researchers determine whether a neutral category has the expected relative location in the ordinal rating scale. For example, many rating scales with neutral categories assume that this category is located in or near the middle of the ordinal scale. Category ordering analyses can help analysts identify the empirical location of the category relative to the other categories in the scale, as interpreted by a particular sample.

Analysts can also use category precision analyses to determine the degree to which the neutral category provides information that is distinct from other categories in the rating scale. Specifically, researchers can use precision analyses from any of the models discussed in this book to evaluate whether the neutral category reflects a distinct range on the latent variable that is large enough to distinguish participants with a meaningfully different level of the latent variable from other categories in the scale.

If category order analyses or category precision analyses indicate that a neutral rating scale category is not functioning in an appropriate way, analysts can consider the suggestions for category disordering and precision discussed earlier. Another solution in this case is to treat neutral responses as missing data. Many measurement models, including Rasch models, can handle missing responses as long as there is sufficient overlap between items and persons (Schumacker, 1999; Wind & Jones, 2019). However, as with any other data manipulation, this solution should be approached cautiously and results from analyses with and without the missing-data version of the neutral category should be fully considered before it is adopted.

Rating scale analysis can also help inform scale development with respect to neutral categories. Specifically, if researchers are constructing a scale and considering whether they should include a neutral category, they may find it useful to pilot-test their instrument with a neutral category. Then, they could use rating scale analyses to examine how the neutral category performs from the perspective of category ordering and category precision. Results from these analyses can inform subsequent versions of the instrument.

160

Resources for Further Study

Interested readers may wish to consult additional resources to learn more about rating scale analysis. This section includes an annotated list of two types of resources: (1) Methodological research on rating scale analysis and (2) Examples of applications of rating scale analysis to real survey data. Resources within each section are organized alphabetically.

Methodological Research on Rating Scale Analysis

> Linacre, J. M. (2002). Optimizing rating scale category effectiveness. *Journal of Applied Measurement, 3*(1), 85–106.

In this article, Linacre discusses rating scale analysis and presents a set of eight guidelines that researchers can use to evaluate rating scale functioning. Along with methods for evaluating rating scales, Linacre provides practical guidance on interpreting the results.

> Wright, B. D., & Masters, G. N. (1982). *Rating scale analysis: Rasch measurement.* MESA Press.

This book includes a detailed presentation of polytomous Rasch models and their use in analyzing item response data. The book includes theoretical and conceptual discussions related to measurement theory as well as technical details about the use of polytomous Rasch models to analyze item responses. Several illustrations are presented that demonstrate the application and interpretation of the models.

Examples of Applications of Rating Scale Analysis to Real Survey Data

> Engelhard, G., & Wind, S. A. (2013). *Rating quality studies using Rasch measurement theory* (Research Report No. 2013–3). The College Board.

This research report summarizes Linacre's (2002) guidelines for evaluating rating scale functioning and uses them to evaluate rating scale functioning for the Advanced Placement Statistics examination. Rating scale analyses are conducted using the RSM and the PCM, and results are compared between the two models.

Kornetti, D. L., Fritz, S. L., Chiu, Y.-P., Light, K. E., & Velozo, C. A. (2004). Rating scale analysis of the Berg balance scale. *Archives of Physical Medicine and Rehabilitation*, *85*(7), 1128–1135. https://doi.org/10.1016/j.apmr.2003.11.019

This article is an example of an empirical application of rating scale analysis based on the RSM to evaluate a measurement instrument related to physical balance. The authors used indicators of rating scale functioning from the RSM to evaluate category ordering and rating scale category precision. The authors also demonstrate how they used the results from rating scale analysis to modify the original rating scale for their instrument to a revised version for future analyses and administrations.

Wesolowski, B. C., Wind, S. A., & Engelhard, G. (2016). Examining rater precision in music performance assessment: An analysis of rating scale structure using the multifaceted Rasch partial credit model. *Music Perception: An Interdisciplinary Journal*, *33*(5), 662–678. https://doi.org/10.1525/mp.2016.33.5.662

This article is an example of an empirical application of rating scale analysis based on the PC-MFR model. The authors use indicators of rating scale functioning from the PC-MFRM to evaluate rating scale category ordering, precision, and comparability for individual raters who scored a music performance assessment.

Wind, S. A., Tsai, C.-L., Grajeda, S. B., & Bergin, C. (2018). Principals' use of rating scale categories in classroom observations for teacher evaluation. *School Effectiveness and School Improvement*, *29*(3), 485–510. https://doi.org/10.1080/09243453.2018.1470989

This article is an example of an empirical application of rating scale analysis to evaluate rating scale category ordering, precision, and comparability in a classroom assessment system. The authors applied methods based on the PC-MFRM to evaluate rating scale functioning for a rubric that was designed to measure teaching effectiveness based on principals' classroom observations.

Hagedoorn, E. I., Paans, W., Jaarsma, T., Keers, J. C., van der Schans, C. P., Luttik, M. L., & Krijnen, W. P. (2018). Translation and psychometric evaluation of the Dutch families importance in nursing care:

Nurses' attitudes scale based on the generalized partial credit model. *Journal of Family Nursing*, *24*(4), 538–562. https://doi.org/10.1177/1074840718810551

In this article, the authors used the GPCM to examine the psychometric properties of a survey designed to measure nurses' attitudes toward family involvement in nursing care. Although the focus of the article was not on rating scale analysis, the authors considered several indicators of rating scale functioning using descriptive statistics and the GPCM.

APPENDIX

Table A.6.1 List of Rating Scale Analysis Indicators

Model	Group of Rating Scale Functioning Indicators	Indicator	Evidence
RSM	Rating Scale Category Ordering	Average participant locations within rating scale categories	Average participant location estimates are nondecreasing as categories increase
		Logit-scale location estimates of rating scale category thresholds	Threshold locations are nondecreasing as categories increase
		Ordering of category probability curves	Probabilities for ratings in lower categories are highest for participants with the lowest latent variable locations and lowest for participants with the highest latent variable locations
	Rating Scale Category Precision	Distance between threshold location estimates on the logit scale	Absolute distances between adjacent-categories threshold estimates are large enough to identify participants with meaningful differences on the latent variable and small enough to provide appropriate distinction among participants
		Distinct category probability curves	The curve associated with each category has a unique range of locations on the logit scale at which it is most probable

(Continued)

Table A.6.1 List of Rating Scale Analysis Indicators *(Continued)*

Model	*Group of Rating Scale Functioning Indicators*	*Indicator*	*Evidence*
		Model-data fit for rating scale categories	There is a close match between expected and observed ratings within individual rating scale categories
PCM	Rating Scale Category Ordering	Average participant locations within rating scale categories for individual items	Average participant location estimates are nondecreasing as categories increase for individual items
		Logit-scale location estimates of rating scale category thresholds for individual items	Threshold locations for individual items are nondecreasing as categories increase
		Ordering of category probability curves for individual items	Probabilities for ratings in lower categories are highest for participants with the lowest latent variable locations and lowest for participants with the highest latent variable locations for individual items
	Rating Scale Category Precision	Distance between threshold location estimates on the logit scale for individual items	Absolute distances between adjacent-categories threshold estimates for individual items are large enough to identify participants with meaningful differences on the latent variable and small enough to provide appropriate distinction among participants

Table A.6.1 List of Rating Scale Analysis Indicators *(Continued)*

Model	Group of Rating Scale Functioning Indicators	Indicator	Evidence
		Distinct category probability curves for individual items	The curve associated with each category has a unique range of locations on the logit scale at which it is most probable for individual items
		Model-data fit for rating scale categories for individual items	There is a close match between expected and observed ratings within individual rating scale categories for individual items
PC-MFRM	Rating Scale Category Ordering	Average participant locations within rating scale categories for elements of explanatory facet(s)	Average participant location estimates are nondecreasing as categories increase for elements of explanatory facet(s)
		Logit-scale location estimates of rating scale category thresholds for elements of explanatory facet(s)	Threshold locations for elements of explanatory facet(s) are nondecreasing as categories increase
		Ordering of category probability curves for elements of explanatory facet(s)	Probabilities for ratings in lower categories are highest for participants with the lowest latent variable locations and lowest for participants with the highest latent variable locations for elements of explanatory facet(s)

(Continued)

Table A.6.1 List of Rating Scale Analysis Indicators *(Continued)*

Model	Group of Rating Scale Functioning Indicators	Indicator	Evidence
	Rating Scale Category Precision	Distance between threshold location estimates on the logit scale for elements of explanatory facet(s)	Absolute distances between adjacent-categories threshold estimates for elements of explanatory facet(s) are large enough to identify participants with meaningful differences on the latent variable and small enough to provide appropriate distinction among participants
		Distinct category probability curves for elements of explanatory facet(s)	The curve associated with each category has a unique range of locations on the logit scale at which it is most probable for elements of explanatory facet(s)
		Model-data fit for rating scale categories for elements of explanatory facet(s)	There is a close match between expected and observed ratings within individual rating scale categories for elements of explanatory facet(s)
	Rating Scale Category Comparability	Comparability of indicators across levels of explanatory facet(s)	Indicators show similar properties across levels of explanatory facet(s)
GPCM	Rating Scale Category Ordering	Average participant locations within item-specific rating scale categories	Average participant location estimates are nondecreasing as categories increase for individual items

Table A.6.1 List of Rating Scale Analysis Indicators *(Continued)*

Model	Group of Rating Scale Functioning Indicators	Indicator	Evidence
		Logit-scale location estimates of item-specific rating scale category thresholds	Threshold locations for individual items are nondecreasing as categories increase
		Ordering of item-specific category probability curves	Probabilities for ratings in lower categories are highest for participants with the lowest latent variable locations and lowest for participants with the highest latent variable locations for individual items
	Rating Scale Category Precision	Distance between item-specific threshold location estimates on the logit scale	Absolute distances between adjacent-categories threshold estimates are large enough to identify participants with meaningful differences on the latent variable and small enough to provide appropriate distinction among participants for individual items
		Distinct item-specific category probability curves	The curve associated with each category has a unique range of locations on the logit scale at which it is most probable for individual items

(Continued)

Table A.6.1 List of Rating Scale Analysis Indicators *(Continued)*

Model	Group of Rating Scale Functioning Indicators	Indicator	Evidence
GRM	Rating Scale Category Ordering	Average participant locations within item-specific rating scale categories	Average participant location estimates are nondecreasing as categories increase for individual items
	Rating Scale Category Precision	Distance between item-specific rating scale category threshold estimates on the logit scale	Absolute value of the differences between item-specific cumulative rating scale category threshold estimates are large enough to identify participants with meaningful differences on the latent variable and small enough to provide appropriate distinction among participants for individual items
		Plots of item-specific cumulative category probabilities	Cumulative category probabilities for a given item are distinct (i.e., do not overlap) for individual items
		Plots of item-specific individual category probabilities	Curve associated with each category has a distinct range of locations on the latent variable at which it is the most probable for individual items
MSA	Rating Scale Category Ordering	Average participant restscores within item-specific rating scale categories	Nondecreasing participant restscores across increasing rating scale categories for individual items

Table A.6.1 List of Rating Scale Analysis Indicators *(Continued)*

Model	Group of Rating Scale Functioning Indicators	Indicator	Evidence
		Counts of item-specific violations of cumulative category monotonicity	Adherence to monotonicity at the category level (infrequent and small violations of monotonicity) for individual items
		Graphical displays of item-specific cumulative category monotonicity	Plots of item-specific cumulative category probabilities are nondecreasing over increasing restscores for individual items
	Rating Scale Category Precision	Distinct item-specific cumulative category probabilities	The distance between cumulative category probabilities is large enough to identify participants with meaningful differences on the latent variable and small enough to provide appropriate distinction among participants for individual items
		Discriminating item-specific cumulative category probabilities	Categories display an appropriate level of distinction among participants with different locations on the latent variable for individual items

TABLES

Table 3.3 Rating Scale Category Calibrations From the PCM

| Item | Rating Scale Category | % of Ratings | Average Participant Location Estimate (θ) | Threshold Location | | Absolute Distance Between Adjacent Threshold Estimates |
				Threshold Estimate (τ)	Standard Error	
1	0	30%	−1.12	N/A	N/A	N/A
	1	40%	−0.89	−1.30	0.08	N/A
	2	26%	−0.54	−0.25	0.08	1.05
	3	4%	−0.02	1.55	0.18	1.80
2	0	50%	−1.11	N/A	N/A	N/A
	1	25%	−0.74	−0.20	0.08	N/A
	2	17%	−0.34	−0.20	0.09	0.00
	3	8%	−0.17	0.40	0.13	0.60
3	0	60%	−1.09	N/A	N/A	N/A
	1	17%	−0.70	0.34	0.08	N/A
	2	13%	−0.49	−0.28[a]	0.09	0.62
	3	10%	−0.04	−0.07	0.13	0.21
4	0	51%	−1.00	N/A	N/A	N/A
	1	22%	−0.67	0.01	0.08	N/A
	2	18%	−0.38	−0.32[a]	0.09	0.33
	3	10%	−0.15	0.31	0.12	0.63
5	0	40%	−1.31	N/A	N/A	N/A
	1	32%	−0.91	−0.86	0.08	N/A
	2	24%	−0.54	−0.47	0.08	0.39
	3	4%	−0.03	1.33	0.18	1.80

Table 3.3 Rating Scale Category Calibrations From the PCM *(Continued)*

| Item | Rating Scale Category | % of Ratings | Average Participant Location Estimate (θ) | Threshold Location | | Absolute Distance Between Adjacent Threshold Estimates |
				Threshold Estimate (τ)	Standard Error	
6	0	51%	−1.15	N/A	N/A	N/A
	1	25%	−0.82	−0.26	0.08	N/A
	2	16%	−0.43	−0.21	0.09	0.05
	3	7%	−0.12	0.47	0.14	0.68
7	0	47%	−1.07	N/A	N/A	N/A
	1	27%	−0.71	−0.30	0.08	N/A
	2	17%	−0.41	−0.12	0.09	0.18
	3	9%	0.02	0.41	0.13	0.53
8	0	44%	−0.84	N/A	N/A	N/A
	1	21%	−0.52	0.05	0.08	N/A
	2	21%	−0.32	−0.40[a]	0.08	0.45
	3	13%	−0.01	0.36	0.11	0.76
9	0	56%	−1.08	N/A	N/A	N/A
	1	22%	−0.71	0.04	0.08	N/A
	2	13%	−0.48	−0.08[a]	0.09	0.12
	3	9%	−0.15	0.05	0.13	0.13
10	0	53%	−1.16	N/A	N/A	N/A
	1	22%	−0.82	−0.08	0.08	N/A
	2	19%	−0.44	−0.51[a]	0.09	0.43
	3	7%	−0.16	0.58	0.14	1.09
11	0	49%	−1.09	N/A	N/A	N/A
	1	30%	−0.72	−0.41	0.08	N/A
	2	13%	−0.29	0.29	0.09	0.70
	3	9%	−0.24	0.12[a]	0.13	0.17
12	0	32%	−0.74	N/A	N/A	N/A
	1	29%	−0.49	−0.55	0.08	N/A

Table 3.3 Rating Scale Category Calibrations From the PCM
(*Continued*)

Item	Rating Scale Category	% of Ratings	Average Participant Location Estimate (θ)	Threshold Location		Absolute Distance Between Adjacent Threshold Estimates
				Threshold Estimate (τ)	Standard Error	
	2	28%	−0.29	−0.33	0.08	0.22
	3	11%	−0.08	0.88	0.12	1.21
13	0	44%	−1.25	N/A	N/A	N/A
	1	27%	−0.98	−0.59	0.08	N/A
	2	24%	−0.54	−0.64[a]	0.08	0.05
	3	5%	−0.29	1.23	0.17	1.87
14	0	55%	−1.17	N/A	N/A	N/A
	1	20%	−0.76	0.05	0.08	N/A
	2	17%	−0.44	−0.49[a]	0.09	0.54
	3	8%	−0.14	0.44	0.14	0.93
15	0	45%	−1.11	N/A	N/A	N/A
	1	29%	−0.84	−0.54	0.08	N/A
	2	19%	−0.49	−0.20	0.09	0.34
	3	6%	−0.21	0.74	0.15	0.94
16	0	37%	−0.80	N/A	N/A	N/A
	1	27%	−0.63	−0.42	0.08	N/A
	2	25%	−0.30	−0.34	0.08	0.08
	3	10%	−0.15	0.76	0.12	1.10
17	0	64%	−1.03	N/A	N/A	N/A
	1	12%	−0.67	0.78	0.08	N/A
	2	12%	−0.43	−0.50[a]	0.09	1.28
	3	12%	−0.17	−0.28	0.12	0.22
18	0	42%	−1.24	N/A	N/A	N/A
	1	36%	−0.82	−0.87	0.08	N/A
	2	17%	−0.51	0.09	0.09	0.96
	3	5%	−0.14	0.78	0.16	0.69

174

Table 3.3   Rating Scale Category Calibrations From the PCM
(Continued)

Item	Rating Scale Category	% of Ratings	Average Participant Location Estimate (θ)	Threshold Location		Absolute Distance Between Adjacent Threshold Estimates
				Threshold Estimate (τ)	Standard Error	
19	0	53%	−1.10	N/A	N/A	N/A
	1	20%	−0.73	0.09	0.08	N/A
	2	18%	−0.44	−0.53[a]	0.09	0.62
	3	9%	−0.11	0.44	0.13	0.97
20	0	45%	−1.13	N/A	N/A	N/A
	1	32%	−0.75	−0.60	0.08	N/A
	2	16%	−0.44	0.12	0.09	0.72
	3	7%	−0.07	0.48	0.14	0.36

[a]Disordered threshold.

Table 4.3   Rating Scale Category Calibrations From the GPCM

Item	Rating Scale Category	% of Ratings	Average Participant Location Estimate (θ)	Threshold Estimate		Absolute Distance Between Adjacent Threshold Estimates
				δ_{ik}	SE	
1	0	30%	−0.54	NA	NA	NA
	1	40%	−0.08	−0.77	0.08	NA
	2	26%	0.50	1.04	0.11	1.82
	3	4%	1.32	4.37	0.21	3.33
2	0	50%	−0.55	NA	NA	NA
	1	25%	0.16	0.88	0.08	NA
	2	17%	0.80	0.91	0.12	0.03
	3	8%	1.12	1.85	0.18	0.93
3	0	60%	−0.45	NA	NA	NA
	1	17%	0.26	1.71	0.08	NA
	2	13%	0.61	0.84[a]	0.12	0.87
	3	10%	1.37	1.20	0.18	0.36

Table 4.3 Rating Scale Category Calibrations From the GPCM *(Continued)*

Item	Rating Scale Category	% of Ratings	Average Participant Location Estimate (θ)	Threshold Estimate δ_{ik}	SE	Absolute Distance Between Adjacent Threshold Estimates
4	0	51%	−0.46	NA	NA	NA
	1	22%	0.12	1.65	0.07	NA
	2	18%	0.57	0.68[a]	0.11	0.97
	3	10%	0.93	1.79	0.16	1.10
5	0	40%	−0.69	NA	NA	NA
	1	32%	0.08	0.04	0.08	NA
	2	24%	0.71	0.68	0.12	0.64
	3	4%	1.57	3.07	0.22	2.39
6	0	51%	−0.50	NA	NA	NA
	1	25%	0.11	0.89	0.08	NA
	2	16%	0.75	1.00	0.12	0.11
	3	7%	1.29	2.05	0.19	1.05
7	0	47%	−0.56	NA	NA	NA
	1	27%	0.13	0.66	0.08	NA
	2	17%	0.62	0.96	0.12	0.30
	3	9%	1.33	1.79	0.18	0.83
8	0	44%	−0.50	NA	NA	NA
	1	21%	0.08	1.57	0.07	NA
	2	21%	0.37	0.16[a]	0.11	1.42
	3	13%	0.87	1.62	0.15	1.46
9	0	56%	−0.43	NA	NA	NA
	1	22%	0.22	1.64	0.08	NA
	2	13%	0.61	1.27[a]	0.12	0.38
	3	9%	1.13	1.39	0.17	0.12
10	0	53%	−0.50	NA	NA	NA
	1	22%	0.11	1.21	0.08	NA
	2	19%	0.75	0.57[a]	0.12	0.64
	3	7%	1.22	2.24	0.18	1.67

176

Table 4.3 Rating Scale Category Calibrations From the GPCM *(Continued)*

Item	Rating Scale Category	% of Ratings	Average Participant Location Estimate (θ)	Threshold Estimate δ_{ik}	SE	Absolute Distance Between Adjacent Threshold Estimates
11	0	49%	−0.51	NA	NA	NA
	1	30%	0.17	0.71	0.07	NA
	2	13%	0.84	1.81	0.12	1.10
	3	9%	0.94	1.44[a]	0.18	0.37
12	0	32%	−0.43	NA	NA	NA
	1	29%	−0.01	0.35	0.08	NA
	2	28%	0.25	0.18[a]	0.10	0.17
	3	11%	0.55	3.77	0.15	3.59
13	0	44%	−0.52	NA	NA	NA
	1	27%	−0.01	0.66	0.08	NA
	2	24%	0.72	0.49[a]	0.11	0.17
	3	5%	1.13	3.54	0.21	3.05
14	0	55%	−0.52	NA	NA	NA
	1	20%	0.24	1.27	0.08	NA
	2	17%	0.77	0.60[a]	0.12	0.66
	3	8%	1.27	1.97	0.18	1.37
15	0	45%	−0.46	NA	NA	NA
	1	29%	0.04	0.71	0.07	NA
	2	19%	0.62	1.14	0.11	0.43
	3	6%	1.05	2.81	0.18	1.66
16	0	37%	−0.38	NA	NA	NA
	1	27%	−0.10	0.95	0.07	NA
	2	25%	0.38	0.39[a]	0.10	0.56
	3	10%	0.60	3.32	0.16	2.93
17	0	64%	−0.38	NA	NA	NA
	1	12%	0.27	3.12	0.08	NA
	2	12%	0.65	0.46[a]	0.12	2.65
	3	12%	1.06	0.73	0.17	0.27

Table 4.3 Rating Scale Category Calibrations From the GPCM
(Continued)

Item	Rating Scale Category	% of Ratings	Average Participant Location Estimate (θ)	Threshold Estimate δ_{ik}	SE	Absolute Distance Between Adjacent Threshold Estimates
18	0	42%	−0.60	NA	NA	NA
	1	36%	0.16	0.04	0.08	NA
	2	17%	0.70	1.48	0.12	1.44
	3	5%	1.30	2.54	0.20	1.07
19	0	53%	−0.50	NA	NA	NA
	1	20%	0.18	1.48	0.08	NA
	2	18%	0.64	0.43[a]	0.12	1.05
	3	9%	1.19	1.97	0.17	1.54
20	0	45%	−0.57	NA	NA	NA
	1	32%	0.16	0.34	0.08	NA
	2	16%	0.67	1.44	0.12	1.09
	3	7%	1.27	2.00	0.17	0.56

[a]Disordered threshold.

Table A.4.2 Rating Scale Category Calibrations From the GRM

Item	Rating Scale Category	% of Ratings	Average Participant Location Within Category	Threshold Estimate δ_{ik}	SE	Absolute Distance Between Adjacent Threshold Estimates
1	0	30%	−1.14	NA	NA	NA
	1	40%	−0.42	−4.66	0.52	NA
	2	26%	0.07	−1.24	0.27	3.41
	3	4%	0.34	1.29	0.27	2.53
2	0	50%	−0.96	NA	NA	NA
	1	25%	−0.68	−2.54	0.20	NA
	2	17%	−0.13	−1.19	0.17	1.36
	3	8%	0.40	0.01	0.11	1.20

Table A.4.2 Rating Scale Category Calibrations From the GRM *(Continued)*

Item	Rating Scale Category	% of Ratings	Average Participant Location Within Category	Threshold Estimate δ_{ik}	SE	Absolute Distance Between Adjacent Threshold Estimates
3	0	60%	−1.22	NA	NA	NA
	1	17%	−0.51	−2.17	0.17	NA
	2	13%	−0.23	−1.21	0.16	0.96
	3	10%	0.33	−0.39	0.11	0.82
4	0	51%	−0.79	NA	NA	NA
	1	22%	−0.49	−2.88	0.28	NA
	2	18%	−0.11	−1.28	0.20	1.60
	3	10%	0.32	−0.03	0.12	1.25
5	0	40%	−1.38	NA	NA	NA
	1	32%	−0.61	−3.12	0.24	NA
	2	24%	−0.05	−0.95	0.18	2.16
	3	4%	0.49	0.45	0.15	1.40
6	0	51%	−1.10	NA	NA	NA
	1	25%	−0.65	−2.79	0.23	NA
	2	16%	−0.10	−1.30	0.19	1.49
	3	7%	0.37	−0.02	0.12	1.28
7	0	47%	−1.16	NA	NA	NA
	1	27%	−0.53	−2.48	0.20	NA
	2	17%	−0.11	−1.12	0.16	1.36
	3	9%	0.41	0.13	0.11	1.25
8	0	44%	−0.74	NA	NA	NA
	1	21%	−0.29	−2.64	0.28	NA
	2	21%	−0.07	−0.91	0.16	1.73
	3	13%	0.33	0.32	0.13	1.23
9	0	56%	−0.98	NA	NA	NA
	1	22%	−0.49	−2.77	0.26	NA
	2	13%	−0.18	−1.53	0.21	1.24
	3	9%	0.30	−0.29	0.13	1.24

Table A.4.2 Rating Scale Category Calibrations From the GRM *(Continued)*

Item	Rating Scale Category	% of Ratings	Average Participant Location Within Category	Threshold Estimate δ_{ik}	SE	Absolute Distance Between Adjacent Threshold Estimates
10	0	53%	−1.06	NA	NA	NA
	1	22%	−0.63	−2.77	0.23	NA
	2	19%	−0.09	−1.16	0.18	1.61
	3	7%	0.36	−0.10	0.12	1.07
11	0	49%	−0.77	NA	NA	NA
	1	30%	−0.73	−2.84	0.25	NA
	2	13%	−0.16	−1.61	0.21	1.23
	3	9%	0.37	0.07	0.12	1.68
12	0	32%	−0.47	NA	NA	NA
	1	29%	−0.22	−4.54	0.70	NA
	2	28%	0.02	−1.00	0.25	3.55
	3	11%	0.25	1.58	0.35	2.58
13	0	44%	−0.97	NA	NA	NA
	1	27%	−0.60	−3.69	0.34	NA
	2	24%	0.00	−1.13	0.21	2.56
	3	5%	0.36	0.31	0.17	1.44
14	0	55%	−1.08	NA	NA	NA
	1	20%	−0.66	−2.48	0.19	NA
	2	17%	−0.20	−1.14	0.16	1.35
	3	8%	0.38	−0.20	0.11	0.94
15	0	45%	−0.88	NA	NA	NA
	1	29%	−0.53	−3.64	0.37	NA
	2	19%	−0.05	−1.49	0.24	2.15
	3	6%	0.32	0.28	0.16	1.78
16	0	37%	−0.50	NA	NA	NA
	1	27%	−0.31	−4.38	0.63	NA
	2	25%	0.07	−1.23	0.27	3.15
	3	10%	0.23	1.06	0.26	2.28

Table A.4.2 Rating Scale Category Calibrations From the GRM (*Continued*)

Item	Rating Scale Category	% of Ratings	Average Participant Location Within Category	Threshold Estimate δ_{ik}	SE	Absolute Distance Between Adjacent Threshold Estimates
17	0	64%	−0.90	NA	NA	NA
	1	12%	−0.55	−2.29	0.20	NA
	2	12%	−0.26	−1.37	0.19	0.93
	3	12%	0.27	−0.67	0.13	0.69
18	0	42%	−1.11	NA	NA	NA
	1	36%	−0.60	−3.27	0.28	NA
	2	17%	−0.14	−1.48	0.22	1.78
	3	5%	0.43	0.39	0.14	1.87
19	0	53%	−1.01	NA	NA	NA
	1	20%	−0.54	−2.60	0.22	NA
	2	18%	−0.15	−1.12	0.17	1.48
	3	9%	0.36	−0.14	0.12	0.98
20	0	45%	−1.10	NA	NA	NA
	1	32%	−0.56	−2.86	0.24	NA
	2	16%	−0.12	−1.39	0.19	1.48
	3	7%	0.40	0.25	0.12	1.64

GLOSSARY

Adjacent-Categories Probability—Probability calculated using responses in pairs of adjacent rating scale categories.

Category Probability Plot—Graphical display that illustrates the conditional probability for a response in individual rating scale categories, given participant locations on the latent variable.

Construct—A variable that is the object of a measurement procedure but is not directly observed, such as depression, empathy, or mathematics achievement. In this book, "construct" is used interchangeably with "latent variable."

Cumulative Probability—Probability associated with a rating in a given category or any higher category ($P(x \geq k)$).

Dichotomous—Scoring in two categories, such as 0 and 1.

Double Monotonicity Model—Mokken Scale Analysis model that requires unidimensionality, local independence, monotonicity, and invariant item ordering.

Generalized Partial Credit Model—Polytomous item response theory model that predicts item responses using participant locations, item locations, item-specific rating scale category thresholds, and item-specific discrimination parameters.

Graded Response Model—Polytomous item response theory model that predicts item responses using participant locations, item locations, item-specific rating scale category thresholds, and item-specific discrimination parameters with a cumulative probability formulation for the threshold parameter.

Guttman Error—For dichotomous items, Guttman errors occur when a participant provides a correct or positive response to a relatively difficult item in combination with an incorrect or negative response to a relatively easier item. For rating scale (polytomous) items, Guttman errors occur when a participant responds in a higher category on a relatively difficult item and also responds in a lower category on a relatively easier item. The practical implication of Guttman errors is that the difficulty order for items does not hold for some participants.

Infit Statistic—Statistic that summarizes the frequency and magnitude of residuals associated with an item or participant, where residuals are weighted by response variance. Because they are weighted, infit statistics are less sensitive to extreme residuals compared to outfit statistics.

Interval Scale of Measurement—Scale of measurement in which units are distinct and ordered, and the difference between scale units is meaningful.

Invariant Item Ordering—Evidence that the relative order of items is the same for all participants.

Item Fit—Description of the alignment between responses associated with individual items and the responses that are expected given parameter estimates from a selected model.

Item Location—Estimate that describes the level of a latent variable required for a correct or positive response to an item. In item response theory applications, item locations are expressed on a log-odds scale (logit scale) metric. Higher locations typically indicate that "more" of a latent variable is required for a correct or positive response.

Item Response Function (IRF)—Description of the relationship between participant locations on the latent variable and the probability for a correct or positive response. IRFs are often displayed visually.

Item Response Theory (IRT)—A paradigm for the development, analysis, and evaluation of measurement instruments (e.g., surveys or tests) for latent variables (i.e., constructs), such as attitudes, abilities, or achievement levels in the social sciences.

Item Step Response Function (ISRF)—Nonparametric representation of the relationship between participant restscores and the probability for a response in or above a rating scale category.

Latent Variable—See "Construct."

Local Independence—Evidence that item responses are statistically independent from one another after controlling for the primary latent variable.

Many-Facet Rasch Model (MFRM)—Rasch model that predicts item responses using participant locations, item locations, and additional researcher-specified explanatory variables. MFRMs can be specified using various formulations of Rasch models.

Mokken Scale Analysis (MSA)—A theory-driven nonparametric approach to scaling items and persons in social science measurement procedures, such as attitude surveys and achievement tests.

Monotone Homogeneity Model—Mokken Scale Analysis model that requires unidimensionality, local independence, and monotonicity.

Monotonicity—Evidence that, as participant locations on the latent variable increase, ordinal item responses are nondecreasing.

Nonparametric Measurement Model—Measurement model that does not impose a specific mathematical formulation on the item response function and maintains an ordinal level of measurement.

Ordinal Scale of Measurement—Scale of measurement in which units are distinct and ordered, but the difference between levels is not meaningful.

Outfit Statistic—Statistic that summarizes the frequency and magnitude of residuals associated with an item or participant. Because they are not weighted, outfit statistics are more sensitive to extreme residuals compared to infit statistics.

Parametric Measurement Model—Measurement model that imposes a specific mathematical formulation on the item response function and produces parameter estimates on an interval-level of measurement.

Partial Credit Model—Rasch model for polytomous data that predicts item responses using participant locations, item locations, and rating scale threshold parameters specific to each item.

Person Fit—Description of the alignment between responses associated with individual participants and the responses that are expected given parameter estimates from a selected model.

Person Location—Level of the person on the latent variable as estimated with a measurement model.

Polytomous—Scoring in three or more categories.

Rasch Measurement Theory—A theoretical framework based on the premise that principles of measurement from the physical sciences should guide measurement procedures in the social and behavioral sciences.

Rasch Model—Measurement model that is theoretically and mathematically aligned with Rasch measurement theory.

Rating Scale Category Ordering—Evidence that higher rating scale categories indicate higher locations on the construct.

Rating Scale Category Precision—Evidence that individual rating scale categories reflect distinct ranges on the construct.

Rating Scale Model—Rasch model for polytomous data that predicts item responses using participant locations, item locations, and one set of rating scale threshold parameters that applies to all items.

Residual—Difference between an observed response and a model-expected response.

Restscore—Total score (i.e., sum score) minus scores on one or more items of interest.

Restscore Group—Group of participants with equal or adjacent restscores. Restscore groups provide additional statistical power for evaluating item properties compared to individual restscores.

Scalability Coefficient—Ratio of observed-to-expected Guttman errors associated with individual items (H_i coefficient), pairs of items (H_{ij} coefficient), or groups of three or more items (H coefficient).

Slope Parameter—Also called discrimination parameter; indicator of the degree to which items distinguish among participants with different locations on the latent variable.

Threshold Parameter—Estimate that describes the location between adjacent rating scale categories on the latent variable. For adjacent-categories models, this value indicates the location where there is an equal probability for a rating in a pair of adjacent categories. For cumulative models, thresholds indicate the location where the probability for a rating in or above a category is equal to 0.5.

Unidimensionality—Evidence that one latent variable is sufficient to explain most of the variation in participant responses to items.

REFERENCES

American Educational Research Association (AERA), American Psychological Association (APA), & National Council on Measurement in Education (NCME). (2014). *Standards for educational and psychological testing*. AERA.

Andrich, D. A. (1978). A rating formulation for ordered response categories. *Psychometrika*, *43*(4), 561–573. https://doi.org/10.1007/BF02293814

Andrich, D. A. (2013). An expanded derivation of the threshold structure of the polytomous Rasch model that dispels any "threshold disorder controversy." *Educational and Psychological Measurement*, *73*(1), 78–124. https://doi.org/10.1177/0013164412450877

Andrich, D. A. (2015). The problem with the step metaphor for polytomous models for ordinal assessments. *Educational Measurement: Issues and Practice*, *34*(2), 8–14. https://doi.org/10.1111/emip.12074

Arias, V. B., Garrido, L. E., Jenaro, C., Martínez-Molina, A., & Arias, B. (2020). A little garbage in, lots of garbage out: Assessing the impact of careless responding in personality survey data. *Behavior Research Methods*, *52*(6), 2489–2505. https://doi.org/10.3758/s13428-020-01401-8

Birnbaum, A. (1968). Some latent trait models and their use in inferring an examinee's ability, part 5. In F. M. Lord, & M. R. Novick (Eds.), *Statistical theories of mental test scores* (pp. 395–479). Addison-Wesley.

Bodner, T. E. (2006). Missing data: Prevalence and reporting practices. *Psychological Reports*, *99*(3), 675–680. https://doi.org/10.2466/PR0.99.3.675-680

Borgers, N., Sikkel, D., & Hox, J. (2004). Response effects in surveys on children and adolescents: The effect of number of response options, negative wording, and neutral mid-point. *Quality and Quantity*, *38*(1), 17–33. https://doi.org/10.1023/B:QUQU.0000013236.29205.a6

Chen, W.-H., & Thissen, D. (1997). Local dependence indexes for item pairs using item response theory. *Journal of Educational and Behavioral Statistics*, *22*(3), 265–289.

Cohen, J. (1968). Weighted kappa: Nominal scale agreement provision for scaled disagreement or partial credit. *Psychological Bulletin*, *70*(4), 213–220. https://doi.org/10.1037/h0026256

Cohen, J. (1969). *Statistical power analysis for the behavioral sciences*. Academic.

Cook, R. M., Fye, H. J., & Wind, S. A. (2021). An examination of the counselor burnout inventory using item response theory in early career postmaster's counselors. *Measurement and Evaluation in Counseling and Development*, *54*(4), 233–250. https://doi.org/10.1080/07481756.2020.1827439

Cosco, T. D., Lachance, C. C., Blodgett, J. M., Co, M., Veronese, N., Wu, Y.-T., & Prina, A. M. (2020). Latent structure of the centre for epidemiologic studies depression scale (CES-D) in older adult pop. *Aging and Mental Health*, *24*(5), 700–704.

Crocker, L., & Algina, J. (1986). *Introduction to classical and modern test theory*. Holt, Rinehart and Winston.

DeAyala, R. J. (2009). *The theory and practice of item response theory*. The Guilford Press.

DeCastellarnau, A. (2018). A classification of response scale characteristics that affect data quality: A literature review. *Quality & Quantity*, *52*(4), 1523–1559. https://doi.org/10.1007/s11135-017-0533-4

Donny, E. C., Denlinger, R. L., Tidey, J. W., Koopmeiners, J. S., Benowitz, N. L., Vandrey, R. G., al'Absi, M., Carmella, S. G., Cinciripini, P. M., Dermody, S. S., Drobes, D. J., Hecht, S. S., Jensen, J., Lane, T., Le, C. T., McClernon, F. J., Montoya, I. D., Murphy, S. E., Robinson, J. D., ... Hatsukami, D. K. (2015). Randomized trial of reduced-nicotine standards for cigarettes. *The New England Journal of Medicine*, *373*(14), 1340–1349. https://doi.org/10.1056/NEJMsa1502403

Embretson, S. E., & Reise, S. P. (2000). *Item response theory for psychologists*. Lawrence Erlbaum Associates, Publishers.

Engelhard, G. (2008). Historical perspectives on invariant measurement: Guttman, Rasch, and Mokken. *Measurement*, *6*(3), 155–189. https://doi.org/10.1080/15366360802197792

Engelhard Jr, G., & Wang, J. (2020). In *Rasch models for solving measurement problems* (*Vol. 187*). SAGE. https://us.sagepub.com/en-us/nam/rasch-models-for-solving-measurement-problems/book267292

Engelhard, G., & Wind, S. A. (2013). *Rating quality studies using Rasch measurement theory*. Research Report No. 2013-3. The College Board.

Engelhard, G., & Wind, S. A. (2018). *Invariant measurement with raters and rating scales: Rasch models for rater-mediated assessments*. Taylor & Francis.

Everett, J. A. C. (2013). The 12 item social and economic conservatism scale (SECS). *PLoS ONE*, *8*(12), 1–11. https://doi.org/10.1371/journal.pone.0082131

Goldammer, P., Annen, H., Stöckli, P. L., & Jonas, K. (2020). Careless responding in questionnaire measures: Detection, impact, and remedies. *The Leadership Quarterly*, *31*(4), 101384. https://doi.org/10.1016/j.leaqua.2020.101384

González, P., Nuñez, A., Merz, E., Brintz, C., Weitzman, O., Navas, E., ... Gallo, L. C. (2017). Measurement properties of the center for epidemiologic studies depression scale (CES-D 10): Findings from HCHS/SOL. *Psychological Assessment*, *29*(4), 372–381. https://doi.org/10.1037/pas0000330

Gordon, R. A., Peng, F., Curby, T. W., & Zinsser, K. M. (2021). An introduction to the many-facet Rasch model as a method to improve observational quality measures with an application to measuring the teaching of emotion skills. *Early Childhood Research Quarterly*, *55*, 149–164. https://doi.org/10.1016/j.ecresq.2020.11.005

Gulliksen, H. (1950). *Theory of mental tests*. Wiley.

Hagedoorn, E. I., Paans, W., Jaarsma, T., Keers, J. C., van der Schans, C. P., Luttik, M. L., & Krijnen, W. P. (2018). Translation and psychometric evaluation of the Dutch families importance in nursing care: Nurses' attitudes scale based on the generalized partial credit model. *Journal of Family Nursing*, *24*(4), 538–562. https://doi.org/10.1177/1074840718810551

Ho, P. (2019). A new approach to measuring overall liking with the many-facet Rasch model. *Food Quality and Preference*, *74*, 100–111. https://doi.org/10.1016/j.foodqual.2019.01.015

Junker, B. W., & Sijtsma, K. (2001). Cognitive assessment models with few assumptions, and connections with nonparametric item response theory. *Applied Psychological Measurement*, *25*(3), 258–272. https://doi.org/10.1177/01466210122032064

Krosnick, J. A., Holbrook, A. L., Berent, M. K., Carson, R. T., Michael Hanemann, W., Kopp, R. J., … Conaway, M. (2002). The impact of no opinion response options on data quality: Non-attitude reduction or an invitation to satisfice? *Public Opinion Quarterly*, *66*(3), 371–403. https://doi.org/10.1086/341394

Ligtvoet, R., Van der Ark, L. A., te Marvelde, J. M., & Sijtsma, K. (2010). Investigating an invariant item ordering for polytomously scored items. *Educational and Psychological Measurement*, *70*(4), 578–595. https://doi.org/10.1177/0013164409355697

Likert, R. (1932). A technique for the measurement of attitudes. *Archives of Psychology*, *22*(140), 55–55.

Linacre, J. M. (1989). *Many-facet Rasch measurement*. MESA Press.

Linacre, J. M. (1994). Sample size and item calibration stability. *Rasch Measurement Transactions*, *7*(4), 328.

Linacre, J. M. (2002). Optimizing rating scale category effectiveness. *Journal of Applied Measurement*, *3*(1), 85–106.

Linacre, J. M. (2016). *Winsteps Rasch measurement (3.92.1)* [Computer software]. Winsteps.com.

Linacre, J. M. (2020). *A user's guide to FACETS: Rasch-model computer programs (3.83.4)* [Computer software]. winsteps.com. http://www.winsteps.com/manuals.htm

Linacre, J. M., & Wright, B. D. (1994). Chi square fit statistics. *Rasch Measurement Transactions*, *8*(2), 360.

Little, R. A., & Rubin, D. B. (2002). In *Statistical analysis with missing data* (2nd ed.). Wiley.

Macêdo, E. A., Appenzeller, S., & Costallat, L. T. L. (2018). Depression in systemic lupus erythematosus: Gender differences in the performance of the beck depression inventory (BDI), center for epidemiologic studies depression scale (CES-D), and hospital anxiety and depression scale (HADS). *Lupus, 27*(2), 179–189. https://doi.org/10.1177/0961203317713142

Mair, P., Hatzinger, R., & Maier, M. J. (2020). *eRm: Extended Rasch modeling (1.0-1)* [Computer software]. https://cran.r-project.org/package=eRm

Masters, G. N. (1982). A Rasch model for partial credit scoring. *Psychometrika, 47*(2), 149–174. https://doi.org/10.1007/BF02296272

Meijer, R. R., & Baneke, J. J. (2004). Analyzing psychopathology items: A Case for nonparametric item response theory modeling. *Psychological Methods, 9*(3), 354–368. https://doi.org/10.1037/1082-989X.9.3.354

Meijer, R. R., & Egberink, I. J. L. (2012). Investigating invariant item ordering in personality and clinical scales: Some empirical findings and a discussion. *Educational and Psychological Measurement, 72*(4), 589–607.

Meijer, R. R., Sijtsma, K., & Smid, N. G. (1990). Theoretical and empirical comparison of the mokken and the Rasch approach to IRT. *Applied Psychological Measurement, 14*(3), 283–298. https://doi.org/10.1177/0146621 69001400306

Mellenbergh, G. J. (1995). Conceptual notes on models for discrete polytomous item responses. *Applied Psychological Measurement, 19*(1), 91–100. https://doi.org/10.1177/014662169501900110

Mokken, R. J. (1971). *A theory and procedure of scale analysis.* De Gruyter.

Molenaar, I. W. (1982). Mokken scaling revisited. *Kwantitative Methoden, 3*(8), 145–164.

Molenaar, I. W. (1997). Nonparametric models for polytomous responses. In W. J. van der Linden & R. K. Hambleton (Eds.), *Handbook of modern item response theory* (pp. 369–380). Springer.

Molenaar, I. W. (2001). Thirty years of nonparametric item response theory. *Applied Psychological Measurement, 25*(3), 295–299.

Molenaar, I. W., & Sijtsma, K. (2000). *MPS5 for windows: A program for mokken scale analysis for polytomous items (5.0)* [Computer software]. ProGAMMA.

Muraki, E. (1997). A generalized partial credit model. In W. J. van der Linden & R. K. Hambleton (Eds.), *Handbook of modern item response theory* (pp. 153–164). Springer. https://doi.org/10.1007/978-1-4757-2691-6_9

Muraki, E., & Muraki, M. (2018). Generalized partial credit model. In W. J. van der Linden (Ed.), *Handbook of item response theory (Vol. 1*, pp. 127–138). CRC Press.

Padilla, J.-L., & Leighton, J. P. (2017). Cognitive interviewing and think aloud methods. In B. D. Zumbo & A. M. Hubley (Eds.), *Understanding and investigating response processes in validation research* (pp. 211–228). Springer International Publishing. https://doi.org/10.1007/978-3-319-56129-5_12

Perreira, K. M., Deeb-Sossa, N., Harris, K. M., & Bollen, K. (2005). What are we measuring? An evaluation of the CES-D across race/ethnicity and immigrant generation*. *Social Forces, 83*(4), 1567–1601. https://doi.org/10.1353/sof.2005.0077

Primi, R., Silvia, P. J., Jauk, E., & Benedek, M. (2019). Applying many-facet Rasch modeling in the assessment of creativity. *Psychology of Aesthetics, Creativity, and the Arts, 13*(2), 176–186. https://doi.org/10.1037/aca0000230

R Core Team. (2021). *R: A language and environment for statistical computing.* R Foundation for Statistical Computing. https://www.R-project.org/

Radloff, L. S. (1977). The CES-D scale: A self-report depression scale for research in the general population. *Applied Psychological Measurement, 1*(3), 385–401. https://doi.org/10.1177/014662167700100306

Ramsay, J. O. (1991). Kernel smoothing approaches to nonparametric item characteristic curve estimation. *Psychometrika, 56*(4), 611–630. https://doi.org/10.1007/BF02294494

Rasch, G. (1960). *Probabilistic models for some intelligence and achievement tests* (Expanded edition, 1980). University of Chicago Press.

Rasch, G. (1961). On general laws and meaning of measurement in psychology. In J. Neyman (Ed.), *Proceedings of the fourth Berkeley Symposium on mathematical statistics and probability* (pp. 321–333). University of California Press.

Rasch, G. (1977). On specific objectivity: An attempt at formalizing the request for generality and validity of scientific statements. *Danish Yearbook of Psychology, 14*, 58–94.

Reckase, M. D. (1979). Unifactor latent trait models applied to multifactor tests: Results and implications. *Journal of Educational and Behavioral Statistics, 4*(3), 207–230. https://doi.org/10.3102/10769986004003207

Rizopoulos, D. (2006). ltm: An R package for latent variable modelling and item response theory analyses. *Journal of Statistical Software, 17*(5), 1–25.

Robitzsch, A., Kiefer, T., & Wu, M. (2020). *TAM: Test analysis modules (3.5-19)* [Computer software]. https://CRAN.R-project.org/package=TAM

Samejima, F. (1969). Estimation of latent ability using a response pattern of graded scores. *Psychometrika Monograph Supplement, 34*(2), No. 17).

Samejima, F. (1997). Graded response model. In W. J. van der Linden & R. K. Hambleton (Eds.), *Handbook of modern item response theory* (pp. 139–152). Springer.

Samejima, F. (2018). Graded response models. In W. J. van der Linden (Ed.), *Handbook of item response theory (Vol. 1*, pp. 95–108). CRC Press.

Santor, D. A., & Ramsay, J. O. (1998). Progress in the technology of measurement: Applications of item response models. *Psychological Assessment, 10*(4), 345–359.

Schumacker, R. E. (1999). Many-facet Rasch analysis with crossed, nested, and mixed designs. *Journal of Outcome Measurement, 3*(4), 323–338.

Seol, H. (2016). Using the bootstrap method to evaluate the critical range of misfit for polytomous Rasch fit statistics. *Psychological Reports, 118*(3), 937–956.

Smith, R. M. (1986). Person fit in the Rasch model. *Educational and Psychological Measurement*, *46*(2), 359–372. https://doi.org/10.1177/0013164486 04600210

Smith, R. M. (2004). Fit analysis in latent trait models. In E. V. Smith & R. M. Smith (Eds.), *Introduction to Rasch measurement* (pp. 73–92). JAM Press.

Toffoli, S. F. L., de Andrade, D. F., & Bornia, A. C. (2016). Evaluation of open items using the many-facet Rasch model. *Journal of Applied Statistics*, *43*(2), 299–316. https://doi.org/10.1080/02664763.2015.1049938

van der Ark, L. A. (2007). Mokken scale analysis in R. *Journal of Statistical Software*, *20*(11), 1–19.

van der Ark, L. A. (2012). New developments in Mokken scale analysis in R. *Journal of Statistical Software*, *48*(5), 1–27.

van der Ark, L. A., & Sijtsma, K. (2005). The effect of missing data imputation on Mokken scale analysis. In L. A. van der Ark, M. A. Croon, & K. Sijtsma (Eds.), *New developments in categorical data analysis for the social and behavioral sciences* (pp. 147–166). Lawrence Erlbaum Associates.

Walker, A. A., & Engelhard, G. (2016). Using person fit and person response functions to examine the validity of person scores in computer adaptive tests. In Q. Zhang (Ed.), *Pacific rim objective measurement symposium (PROMS) 2015 conference proceedings* (pp. 369–381). Springer. https://doi.org/10.1007/ 978-981-10-1687-5_24

Walker, A. A., Jennings, J. K., & Engelhard, G. (2018). Using person response functions to investigate areas of person misfit related to item characteristics. *Educational Assessment*, *23*(1), 47–68. https://doi.org/10.1080/10627197.2017. 1415143

Wang, Y., & Wind, S. A. (2020). Psychometric evaluation of a new internalization of learning motivation (ILM) scale. *Current Psychology*, *41*, 3888–3905. https://doi.org/10.1007/s12144-020-00909-8

Weijters, B., Cabooter, E., & Schillewaert, N. (2010). The effect of rating scale format on response styles: The number of response categories and response category labels. *International Journal of Research in Marketing*, *27*(3), 236–247. https://doi.org/10.1016/j.ijresmar.2010.02.004

Wesolowski, B. C., Wind, S. A., & Engelhard, G. (2015). Rater fairness in music performance assessment: Evaluating model-data fit and differential rater functioning. *Musicae Scientiae*, *19*(2), 147–170. https://doi.org/10.1177/ 1029864915589014

Wesolowski, B. C., Wind, S. A., & Engelhard, G. (2016). Examining rater precision in music performance assessment: An analysis of rating scale structure using the multifaceted Rasch partial credit model. *Music Perception: An Interdisciplinary Journal*, *33*(5), 662–678. https://doi.org/10.1525/ mp.2016.33.5.662

Wetzel, E., & Carstensen, C. H. (2014). Reversed thresholds in partial credit models: A reason for collapsing categories? *Assessment*, *21*(6), 765–774. https://doi.org/10.1177/1073191114530775

Wilson, M. (2011). Some notes on the term: "Wright map." *Rasch Measurement Transactions, 25*(3), 1331.

Wind, S. A. (2014). Examining rating scales using Rasch and Mokken models for rater-mediated assessments. *Journal of Applied Measurement, 15*(2), 100–132.

Wind, S. A. (2016). Adjacent-categories Mokken models for rater-mediated assessments. *Educational and Psychological Measurement, 77*(2), 330–350. https://doi.org/10.1177/0013164416643826

Wind, S. A. (2020). Applying Mokken scaling techniques to incomplete rating designs for educational performance assessments. *Measurement: Interdisciplinary Research and Perspectives, 18*(1), 23–36. https://doi.org/10.1080/15366367.2019.1644093

Wind, S. A., Jami, P. Y., & Mansouri, B. (2018a). Exploring the psychometric properties of the empathy quotient for Farsi speakers. *Current Psychology, 40.* https://doi.org/10.1007/s12144-018-9938-z

Wind, S. A., & Jones, E. (2019). The effects of incomplete rating designs in combination with rater effects. *Journal of Educational Measurement, 56*(1), 76–100. https://doi.org/10.1111/jedm.12201

Wind, S. A., Mansouri, B., & Jami, P. Y. (2019). Examining the psychometric properties of a questionnaire to investigate Iranian EFL learners' preferences for isolated and integrated form-focused grammar instruction. *Journal of Applied Measurement, 20*(1), 45–65.

Wind, S. A., & Patil, Y. J. (2016). Exploring incomplete rating designs with Mokken scale analysis. *Educational and Psychological Measurement, 78*(2), 1–24. https://doi.org/10.1177/0013164416675393

Wind, S. A., Tsai, C.-L., Grajeda, S. B., & Bergin, C. (2018b). Principals' use of rating scale categories in classroom observations for teacher evaluation. *School Effectiveness and School Improvement, 29*(3), 485–510. https://doi.org/10.1080/09243453.2018.1470989

Wolfe, E. W. (2013). A bootstrap approach to evaluating person and item fit to the Rasch model. *Journal of Applied Measurement, 14*(1), 1–9.

Wright, B. D., & Masters, G. N. (1982). *Rating scale analysis: Rasch measurement.* MESA Press.

Wright, B. D., & Mok, M. M. C. (2004). An overview of the family of Rasch measurement models. In E. V. Smith & R. M. Smith (Eds.), *Introduction to Rasch measurement* (pp. 1–24). JAM Press.

Wu, M., & Adams, R. J. (2013). Properties of Rasch residual fit statistics. *Journal of Applied Measurement, 14*(4), 339–355.

Yaghoubi Jami, P., & Wind, S. A. (2022). Evaluating psychometric properties of the Farsi version of the interpersonal reactivity index. *Research on Social Work Practice.* https://doi.org/10.1177/10497315221089322

Yen, W. M. (1984). Effects of local item dependence on the fit and equating performance of the three-parameter logistic model. *Applied Psychological Measurement, 8*(2), 125–145. https://doi.org/10.1177/014662168400800201

INDEX

A

Adjacent categories probability formulation, 25, 110
Adjacent rating scale category thresholds, 57 (figure)
Akaike Information Criteria (AIC), 93
Attitude surveys, 1, 4, 125

B

Bayesian Information Criteria (BIC), 93
Bernoulli (binomial) trials, 56

C

Category ordering indices
  average participant locations, 72–73, 72 (table)–73 (table)
  category probability curves, 74
  logit-scale location estimates of, 73–74
  Partial Credit Model (PCM), 61–66
Category probability curves, 53–54, 53 (figure)
  ordering of, 63–66, 64 (figure)–65 (figure)
Category probability plots
  cumulative, 112, 141 (figure)
  interpretation of, 106, 106 (figure)
Center for Epidemiological Studies Depression (CES-D) scale, 10, 17, 18, 19
  Graded Response Model (GRM), 104, 106 (figure)
  Guttman errors, 133
  invariant item ordering (IIO), 135
  item stems, 16 (table)

local independence, 20, 31
mean square error (MSE) statistics, 33
Mokken Scale Analysis (MSA), 132 (table)
monotonicity, 129
non-Rasch models, 87
Partial Credit Model (PCM), 40–41
PC-MFRM, 44–45
polytomous Rasch models, 24
Rating Scale Model (RSM), 27–29
standard errors (SE) for, 52
unidimensionality, 30
Wright map, 34, 37 (figure)
Cumulative probability formulation, 103, 111

D

DeAyala, R. J., 29
Dichotomous Rasch model. *See also* Rating Scale Model (RSM)
  equation for, 21
  exponent format of, 23
  item response functions (IRFs), 22, 22 (figure)
  probability, 23
Distinct category probability curves, 58, 78
  for individual items, 67
Donny, E. C., 17, 18
Double monotonicity model (DMM), 127
  polytomous, 134–135

E

Extended Rasch Models (eRm), 59

193

F

Facets software, 29, 31
Partial Credit Model (PCM), 40

G

Generalized Partial Credit Model
(GPCM), 4, 9, 151
Akaike Information Criteria
(AIC), 93
Bayesian Information Criteria
(BIC), 93
equation for, 90
item-level fit statistics, 94
Marginal Maximum Likelihood
Estimation (MMLE), 93
overall item estimates, 95 (table)
person location estimates, 91
rating scale analysis with, 91–93,
92 (table)
rating scale category calibrations,
119 (table)–121 (table), 174
(table)–177 (table)
Test Analysis Modules (TAM), 93
Graded Response Model (GRM), 4,
27, 151
category probabilities, 106, 106
(figure)
cumulative category probabilities,
105, 105 (figure)
equation for, 104
item-category parameters, 104
item-level fit analysis, 109
overall item estimates, 110 (table)
probability, 104
rating scale analysis with, 107–108,
107 (table)–108 (table)
rating scale category calibrations,
122 (table)–124 (table), 177
(table)–180 (table)
GRM. *See* Graded Response Model
(GRM)
Guttman errors, 133
frequency of, 134
practical implication of, 133

I

IIO. *See* Invariant item ordering
(IIO)
Infit mean square error (MSE)
statistics, 32–33
Invariant item ordering (IIO)
CES-D scale, 135
double monotonicity model,
134–135
test for, 135, 136 (figure)
Invariant measurement, 19, 23
requirements for, 20
IRT. *See* Item response theory (IRT)
Item monotonicity plots, 130 (figure)
Item-person map, 34
Item response functions (IRFs), 22,
22 (figure)
Item response theory (IRT)
defined, 2
educational assessment, 3
multidimensional, 8
nonparametric, 9, 11, 125
non-Rasch, 16 (*See also* Non-
Rasch item response theory
models)
parametric, 125
polytomous, 88–93
Rasch models, 21
rating scale data, 4
unidimensionality, 3
Item-specific category probability
curves, 98–99
Item-specific fit analysis, 31–34
Item-specific residuals, 31
Item Step Response Functions
(ISRFs), 129

J

Joint Maximum Likelihood
Estimation (JMLE), 29

K

Kappa coefficients, 126
Kernel smoothing, 126

L

Latent trait theory, 2. *See also* Item response theory (IRT)
Latent variables, 2, 3
concept of, 3, 3 (figure)
Rating Scale Model (RSM), 28
Likert-type rating scales, 1, 4
five ordered categories, 5, 5 (figure)
Linacre, J. M., 41, 52, 56, 66, 78, 160
Local independence, 20, 23
double monotonicity model, 134
item-specific residuals, 31
monotone homogeneity model, 128

M

Many-Facet Rasch Model (MFRM), 19
logit-scale locations, 41
PC-MFRM, 43–45
rating scale functioning, 43
RS-MFRM, 43
Marginal Maximum Likelihood Estimation (MMLE), 93
Mean square error (MSE) statistics
infit, 32–33
outfit, 32
MFRM. *See* Many-Facet Rasch Model (MFRM)
Model-data fit analysis, 29–30
rating scale categories, 58–59, 60 (figure)
Mokken Scale Analysis (MSA), 4
defined, 126
invariant item ordering, 135–137
kappa coefficients, 126
kernel smoothing, 126
monotone homogeneity model (MHM), 127–129
monotonicity, 129–133, 130 (figure), 132 (table)
polytomous double monotonicity model, 134–135
Rasch measurement theory and, 127

rating scale analysis with, 136–137, 137 (table)
rating scale category results, 147 (table)–149 (table)
scalability, 133–134
Molenaar, I. W., 128, 134
Monotone homogeneity model (MHM), 127
polytomous, 127–129
Monotonicity, 129–133, 130 (figure), 132 (table)
MSA. *See* Mokken Scale Analysis (MSA)

N

Nonparametric measurement models
defined, 125
Mokken Scale Analysis (MSA), 126–137
rating scale category functioning indices, 126, 126 (table)
rating scale category ordering, 138–140
rating scale category precision, 140–144
Non-Rasch item response theory models, 87
characteristics, 87
Graded Response Model (GRM), 104–108
polytomous IRT models, 88–93
rating scale category functioning indices, 88 (table)
rating scale category ordering, 96–99, 110–111
rating scale category precision, 99–103, 111–117

O

One-parameter logistic model, 21
One-sample Z-test, 131
Outfit mean square error (MSE) statistics, 32

P

Partial Credit Many-Facet Rasch Model (PC-MFRM)
category ordering indices, 72–74
comparability, 71
rating scale category precision, 74–82
rating scale functioning, 71
rating scale thresholds, 71
Partial Credit Model (PCM), 19, 27
application of, 40–41
average participant locations, 61–63, 62 (table)
category probability curves, 63–66, 64 (figure)–65 (figure)
item response data, 40
logit-scale location estimates of, 63
log-odds form, 39
rating scale category, 39–40
rating scale category calibrations, 84 (table)–86 (table), 171 (table)–174 (table)
rating scale category comparability, 70–71
rating scale category precision, 66–67
vs. Rating Scale Model (RSM), 38
threshold locations, 39
PCM. *See* Partial Credit Model (PCM)
Person-specific fit analysis, 31–34
Poisson counts Rasch models, 43
Polytomous double monotonicity model, 134–135
Polytomous item response theory models, 88
Generalized Partial Credit Model (GPCM), 90–91
item discrimination, 90
slope parameters, 89 (figure)
Polytomous monotone homogeneity model, 127
local independence, 128
monotonicity, 128

restscores, 128
unidimensionality, 128
Polytomous Rasch models, 23, 48.
See also Rating Scale Model (RSM)
adjacent categories probability formulation, 25
average participant locations, 50–51
category probability curves, 53–54, 53 (figure)
distinct category probability curves, 58
expected ratings, 24, 25 (figure)
exponent form of, 26
item responses, 25
model-data fit for, 58–59, 60 (figure)
rating scale category comparability, 60–61
rating scale category functioning, 49 (table)
rating scale category ordering, 50
rating scale category precision, 54–55
rating scale category probability curves, 24, 24 (figure)
rating scale category threshold parameter, 26, 51–53
threshold location estimates, 55–57, 57 (figure)
Psychometrics, 15

R

Rasch, G., 19
Rasch measurement theory, 19–28, 150
Mokken Scale Analysis (MSA) and, 127
Wright maps, 34
Rasch models, 2, 9
dichotomous, 21
item- and person-specific fit analysis, 31–34

item response theory (IRT), 21
local independence, 31
missing data, 11
model-data fit, 29–30
Poisson counts, 43
polytomous, 23–27
rating scale analysis, 15–16, 27–38
Rating Scale Model (RSM), 27–29
unidimensionality, 30–31
Rating scale analysis
applications of, 160–162
defined, 5, 150
indicators, 163 (table)–169 (table)
indices used in, 1, 1 (table)
individual categories, 7, 7 (figure)
item sample size, 10
methodological research, 160
missing data, 10–11
neutral category, 159
overall item difficulty estimates, 6
overall modeling goals, 153–154
Partial Credit Many-Facet Rasch
Model (PC-MFRM), 71–82
with Partial Credit Model (PCM),
61–71
participant sample size, 9
polytomous Rasch models. See
Polytomous Rasch models
practical goals for, 154–155
Rasch models. See Rasch models
rating scale categories, 8–9
with Rating Scale Model (RSM),
48–61
requirements for, 8
researchers selection, 11–15, 12
(table)–14 (table)
scale categories, 156–158
Rating scale categories
comparability, 1
number of, 8–9
precision, 1
Rating scale category comparability,
60–61, 70–71

Rating scale category ordering, 50,
110–111
average participant locations,
96–97
average participant restscores,
138
cumulative category monotonicity,
139–140
item-specific category probability
curves, 98–99
item-specific violations of category
monotonicity, 139
logit-scale location estimates,
97–98
Rating scale category precision,
54–55
cumulative category probabilities,
112–117, 113 (figure)–116
(figure)
cumulative probability
formulation, 103
discriminating item-specific
cumulative category
probabilities, 144
distinct cumulative category
probabilities, 140–144, 141
(figure)–142 (figure)
distinct item-specific category
probability curves, 100–103,
101 (figure)–102 (figure)
distinct rating scale category
probability curves, 67
graphical model-data fit displays,
67, 68 (figure)–69 (figure)
item-specific threshold location
estimates, 99–100
polytomous IRT models, 103
rating scale category threshold
estimates, 111–112
threshold location estimates,
66–67, 74–78
Rating scale category thresholds,
51–53

logit-scale location estimates of,
63, 73–74
Rating scale data, 4
Mokken models for, 127–137
Rating scale functioning, 1, 2, 15
comparability of, 71
Many-Facet Rasch Model
(MFRM), 43
Rating Scale Model (RSM), 4, 19,
27, 48–61
application of, 28–29
category probability curves, 53
(figure)
Center for Epidemiological Studies
Depression (CES-D) scale,
28–29
expected and empirical item
response function, 60 (figure)
latent variable, 28
rating scale category calibrations,
51 (table)
results, 34–38, 35 (figure)–37
(figure), 39 (figure)
Rating Scale model formulation of
the MFRM (RS-MFRM), 43
Residuals, 30, 32
item-specific, 31
variance of, 31
Restscores, 128
R software packages, 15, 31

S
Scalability, 133–134
Slope parameters, 88–93
Specific objectivity, 19
Standard errors (SE), 52
Statistical software, 15

T
Test Analysis Modules (TAM), 59, 93
Threshold disordering, 52
Threshold parameter, 26, 39, 91, 110

U
Unidimensionality, 3, 20, 23
double monotonicity model, 134
monotone homogeneity model, 128
proportion of variance, 30–31

V
Variable map, 34

W
Wind, S. A., 19, 138
Wright maps, 34, 37 (figure), 41
Partial Credit Model (PCM), 42
(figure)
PC-MFRM, 46 (figure)

Y
Yaghoubi Jami, P., 19